The Question of Providence

The Question of Providence

Charles M. Wood

Westminster John Knox Press
LOUISVILLE • LONDON

BT
135
.W66
2008

© 2008 Charles M. Wood

Unless otherwise indicated, Scripture quotations are from the New Revised Standard Version of the Bible, copyright © 1989 by the Division of Christian Education of the National Council of the Churches of Christ in the U.S.A., and are used by permission.

Scripture quotations marked RSV are from the Revised Standard Version of the Bible, copyright © 1946, 1952, 1971, and 1973 by the Division of Christian Education of the National Council of the Churches of Christ in the U.S.A., and are used by permission.

Chapter 1 was originally published as "The Question of the Doctrine of Providence" in *Theology Today* 49 (July 1992):209–24. Reprinted with minor revisions with the permission of the editor of *Theology Today*. All rights reserved. Chapter 4 was originally published as "How Does God Act?" in *International Journal of Systematic Theology* 1 (1999):138–52. Reprinted with minor revisions and a new title with the permission of Blackwell Publishing Ltd. All rights reserved.

Book design by Sharon Adams
Cover design by Lisa Buckley

First edition
Published by Westminster John Knox Press
Louisville, Kentucky

This book is printed on acid-free paper that meets the American National Standards Institute Z39.48 standard. ♾

PRINTED IN THE UNITED STATES OF AMERICA

08 09 10 11 12 13 14 15 16 — 10 9 8 7 6 5 4 3 2 1

Library of Congress Cataloging-in-Publication Data

Wood, Charles Monroe.
    The question of providence / Charles M. Wood. — 1st ed.
        p. cm.
    ISBN 978-0-664-23255-9 (alk. paper)
    1. Providence and government of God. I. Title.

BT135.W66 2008
231'.5—dc22

2007046591

Contents

Acknowledgments

A version of chapter 1 originally appeared under the same title in *Theology Today*, and a version of chapter 4 (under the title "How Does God Act?") appeared in the *International Journal of Systematic Theology.* I thank the editors of both journals for permission to republish in this form. I also thank the members of the faculty symposium at Perkins School of Theology, the Systematic Theology Working Group at the eleventh Oxford Institute of Methodist Theological Studies, and the Systematic Theology Seminar of Cambridge University for their helpful discussions of earlier drafts of chapters 1, 3, and 4, respectively.

A research grant from the Lilly Endowment supported my work on this project at a critical stage, and I wish to record my deep gratitude to the endowment and to Dr. Craig Dykstra, its vice president for Religion, for this assistance and encouragement.

Introduction

*I*n the days following the terrorist attacks of September 11, 2001, a pastor in New Orleans wrote to tell me of a message she had just seen on a sign outside a neighboring church there:

There Is No Problem Bigger Than God.

The message admits of more than one interpretation. Presumably its writer, in those anxious days, intended to convey the assurance that there is no problem that God cannot handle: no problem is too big for God. It was a less reassuring construal of the message that registered with my wary correspondent, however: God is the biggest problem of all. God is, as it were, the mother of all problems.

To be sure, this is a strained and, one might even think, perverse reading of the sign's message. Its writer certainly neither said nor meant, "There is no bigger problem than God." Still, I doubt that my correspondent was the only reader of the sign to see this meaning in it, particularly in the aftermath of September 11.

"To suffer in the Bible means to suffer because of *God*; to sin, to sin against *God*; to doubt, to doubt of *God*; to perish, to perish at the hand of *God*." So Karl Barth forcefully reminded his hearers at a conference of rural Swiss pastors in 1922, urging them not to underestimate the depth and seriousness of the unspoken theological questions people bring with them to church on Sunday mornings.[1] James A. Sanders has written insightfully of what he calls the "monotheizing"

---

1. Karl Barth, "The Need and Promise of Christian Preaching," *The Word of God and the Word of Man*, trans. Douglas Horton (New York: Harper & Row, 1957), 119.

dynamic in the biblical writings: the way the canonical materials, taken together, pursue a vision of "the Integrity of Reality."[2] Those for whom these writings are Scripture find themselves facing a perennial task: everything that happens must ultimately in some way be referred to God. It was his own mindfulness of this dynamic and of the difficulties it imposes that led H. Richard Niebuhr to write in *The Purpose of the Church and Its Ministry* that the human problem is "how to love the One on whom [we are] completely, absolutely dependent; who is the Mystery behind the mystery of human existence. . . . It is the problem of reconciliation to the One from whom death proceeds as well as life. . . . It is the problem that arises in its acutest form when life itself becomes a problem."[3]

The point is succinctly stated by Daniel Hardy and David Ford: "Coping with God and his generosity is the central task of Christian faith."[4] To identify not just God, but specifically God's generosity, as a problem to be coped with may seem strange, until one remembers how prominent in the Bible is this very theme. The complaint of Jeremiah 12 brings out some features of the problem:

> Righteous art thou, O LORD, when I complain to thee;
>   yet I would plead my case before thee.
> Why does the way of the wicked prosper?
>   Why do all who are treacherous thrive?
> Thou plantest them, and they take root;
>   they grow and bring forth fruit.
>   (Jer. 12:1–2 [RSV])

Numerous parables in the Synoptic Gospels—for example, those of the Prodigal Son, and of the Laborers in the Vineyard—force their

---

2. James A. Sanders, *Canon and Community: A Guide to Canonical Criticism* (Philadelphia: Fortress Press, 1984), 56–60.

3. H. Richard Niebuhr, *The Purpose of the Church and Its Ministry* (New York: Harper & Row, 1956), 36–37. Earlier in the book, Niebuhr describes theological education as "the nurture of men and women whose business in life it will be to help men to see their immediate perplexities, joys and sufferings in the light of an ultimate meaning, to live as citizens of the inclusive society of being, and to relate their present choices to first and last decisions made about them in the totality of human history by Sovereign Power" (2–3). Sanders (*Canon and Community,* 58) counts Niebuhr among the few in Christian history who have consistently struggled to "monotheize" rather than succumb to the temptation to "fragmentize" truth and reality.

4. Daniel W. Hardy and David F. Ford, *Praising and Knowing God* (Philadelphia: Westminster Press, 1984), 71.

hearers and readers to confront the divine generosity, especially to the undeserving and the wicked, in ways that still challenge. The words of Jesus in Matt. 5:44–45 state the point plainly: "'But I say to you, Love your enemies and pray for those who persecute you, so that you may be children of your Father in heaven; for he makes his sun rise on the evil and on the good, and sends rain on the righteous and on the unrighteous.'"

In Christian discourse and life, the problem of God and of God's generosity has traditionally been addressed by the doctrine of providence. But on the whole, the doctrine has functioned to resolve the problem by denying its existence and by portraying a universal order in which everything that happens is specifically arranged by God to serve God's good purposes. The wicked may prosper now (and if they do, it is because God wills it for some good end), but eventually they will receive their punishment; the good may suffer now (and, likewise, if they do, it is because God wills it for some good end), but eventually they will receive their reward. Despite appearances, all is well.

This doctrine has fallen on hard times. Although it is still invoked on special occasions, it has long since ceased to operate as a guiding principle in the lives of many, if not most, Christians. What Paul Ricoeur has termed "the death of the God of providence"[5] is a fact of Christian existence as well as of that of Western culture at large. Clergy and laity alike may draw on the traditional language in situations of crisis simply because they have nothing to take its place, but when they do, they often discover both that they no longer "own" the language in any real sense and that its use creates more difficulties than it removes.

In an essay published in 1963 on the state of the doctrine of providence, Langdon Gilkey characterized the doctrine as "a rootless, disembodied ghost, flitting from footnote to footnote, but rarely finding secure lodgement in sustained theological discourse."[6] The doctrine in its received form had been seriously undermined by the rise of

---

5. Paul Ricoeur, "Religion, Atheism, and Faith," in *The Conflict of Interpretations: Essays in Hermeneutics*, ed. Don Ihde (Evanston, IL: Northwestern University Press, 1974), 455.

6. Langdon B. Gilkey, "The Concept of Providence in Contemporary Theology," *The Journal of Religion* 43 (1963): 171. I have attempted an assessment of the present state of the question in Charles M. Wood, "Providence," *The Oxford Handbook of Systematic Theology*, ed. John Webster, Kathryn Tanner, and Iain Torrance (New York: Oxford University Press, 2007), 91–104.

modern scientific thinking and by the growth of historical consciousness since the late eighteenth century. It had a rebirth of sorts as liberal Christians embraced evolutionary thought in the late nineteenth
century and saw God's guiding hand in the unfolding of creation and
particularly in human progress. Though this modern form of the doctrine would have been difficult to reconcile with the older version in
many respects, the two had similar functions. With the First World
War, however, faith in progress became increasingly difficult to sustain, and providence found no other theological niche to occupy. The
doctrine was dutifully mentioned in textbooks and in popular literature, but it received little serious examination or constructive restatement. Gilkey's account of the reasons for this neglect is still largely
persuasive, and if (as seems to be the case) we are currently witnessing a revival of serious theological interest in the notion of providence, the revival may be evidence of the importance of some fairly
recent theological and cultural changes.

In this book, I hope to contribute to the renewal of reflection on
the Christian doctrine of providence in two specific ways. First, by
applying and extending recent thinking about the character and function of doctrine in religious communities, I hope to shed light on several points regarding the doctrine of providence. This line of inquiry
should help us understand what a Christian doctrine of providence is
for—that is, what work it is supposed to do—and how its adequacy
might be assessed. It should also illuminate some features of the
history of the doctrine of providence. Second, by proposing a reorientation of the doctrine around the central Trinitarian and christological commitments of Christian faith and indicating what such a
reorientation might involve, I hope to point the way toward a doctrine of providence that would have a more evident coherence with
the gospel than traditional doctrines of providence have managed to
display.

The book has five chapters. In the first, I attempt to identify the
question to which the Christian doctrine of providence may be con-
strued as an answer, and also to consider what would make such an
answer a *doctrine* and what would make it *Christian*. The second
chapter offers a detailed exposition of what was perhaps the last thorough treatment of the doctrine of providence to enjoy wide currency

in the English-speaking world, William Sherlock's *Discourse Concerning the Divine Providence* (1694). Sherlock's treatise represents the doctrine that lingers, at least in fragments, in the memory of church and culture, and retrieving it in fuller form for a thoughtful reexamination is an important step toward clarity. The third chapter explores how this sort of doctrine of providence achieved its standing, considers the reasons for its decline, and uncovers some principles that might inform an alternative vision of God's engagement with the world and our lives.

The remaining two chapters are more constructive in intent. Chapter 4, by taking up the question of how God acts, aims to set out the Trinitarian "grammar" of a Christian understanding of God's involvement in what goes on. Chapter 5 relates that grammar to the christological heart of such an understanding and suggests some implications for doctrinal reconstruction.

Chapter 1

The Question of the Doctrine of Providence

*W*hat is the Christian doctrine of providence?

One way to answer that question would be to bring forth some representative statement of the doctrine from Christian tradition. One might, for example, turn to the Heidelberg Catechism—called "the most ecumenical of the confessions of the Protestant Churches"— which has as its question 27, *"What do you understand by the providence of God?"* The answer runs,

> The almighty and ever-present power of God whereby he still upholds, as it were by his own hand, heaven and earth together with all creatures, and rules in such a way that leaves and grass, rain and drought, fruitful and unfruitful years, food and drink, health and sickness, riches and poverty, and everything else, come to us not by chance but by his fatherly hand.[1]

This, or something very close to it, has been widely accepted as the Christian doctrine of providence for a very long time. Whatever exists, exists because God wills to sustain it; and whatever happens, happens ultimately because God directs it. Whatever befalls us, whether it seems good or ill, is to be seen as "provided" by God.

Most of the treatises on providence before the onset of modernity, and a good many right up to the present day, have been devoted to

---

1. The quotation concerning the ecumenicity of the Heidelberg Catechism is from the translators' introduction to the edition from which these citations are taken: *The Heidelberg Catechism*, trans. Allen O. Miller and M. Eugene Osterhaven (Philadelphia: United Church Press, 1962).

explicating and defending such a view and to encouraging Christians to adopt an attitude much like that commended by the Heidelberg Catechism in its very next question (#28): *"What advantage comes from acknowledging God's creation and providence?"*

We learn that we are to be patient in adversity, grateful in the midst of blessing, and to trust our faithful God and Father for the future, assured that no creature shall separate us from his love, since all creatures are so completely in his hand that without his will they cannot even move.

But is this, in fact, the Christian doctrine of providence? Certainly it is believed to be so by a great number of people: by Christians who believe what this doctrinal statement teaches and find themselves comforted or troubled (or both) by it; by Christians who do not believe it but feel that it is in some sense what they *ought* to be believing as Christians, and who thus experience a certain conflict in their Christian identity as a result; and by non-Christians who simply take it to be the common teaching of Christian churches on this point.

However, the fact that a great many people are convinced that this is the Christian doctrine of providence does not make it so.

What *would* make it so? What would qualify this, or any other statement, as a valid statement of the Christian doctrine of providence? It is to that question that this first chapter is directed.

The inquiry will have two stages. The first will be an exploration of the character and function of Christian doctrine. The second will turn more specifically to the question of the doctrine of providence. The chapter will conclude with some brief reflections on the importance of pursuing the question.

The Question of Christian Doctrine

"What the church of Jesus Christ believes, teaches, and confesses on the basis of the word of God: this is Christian doctrine."[2] So runs the opening sentence of the first volume of Jaroslav Pelikan's five-volume

---

2. Jaroslav Pelikan, *The Christian Tradition: A History of the Development of Doctrine*, vol. 1: *The Emergence of the Catholic Tradition* (Chicago: University of Chicago Press, 1971), 1.

history of doctrine. The phrase "believes, teaches, and confesses" is borrowed from the Lutheran *Formula of Concord*, in which nearly every major affirmation begins with "We believe, teach, and confess that. . . ."[3] Pelikan's use of the phrase is part of his effort to open up a richer notion of "doctrine" than the one with which we operate when we fall into the common tendency to identify "doctrine" with the officially promulgated teachings of the church. He proceeds to suggest three corresponding aspects of Christian doctrine:

> Without setting rigid boundaries, we shall identify what is "believed" as the form of Christian doctrine present in the modalities of devotion, spirituality, and worship; what is "taught" as the content of the word of God extracted by exegesis from the witness of the Bible and communicated to the people of the church through proclamation, instruction, and churchly theology; and what is "confessed" as the testimony of the church, both against false teaching from within and against attacks from without, articulated in polemics and in apologetics, in creed and in dogma.[4]

The distinctions Pelikan introduces here are helpful, but they deserve to be sharpened and extended.

Doctrine and Teaching

"Doctrine" means "teaching." But "teaching" can refer either to an activity or to what is normally taken to be conveyed from teacher to learner through that activity: information, insight, wisdom, skill. In many religious communities, to have "received the doctrine" means to have undergone the sort of instruction that equips one with the knowledge and abilities pertinent to being a competent participant in the community and, perhaps, to being a teacher of others in turn—a bearer of the tradition.

It is important to keep in mind that what is conveyed through such instruction is ordinarily not simply a body of statements to be memorized or written down and learned, but rather a whole set of attitudes

---

3. *The Book of Concord: The Confessions of the Evangelical Lutheran Church*, trans. and ed. Theodore G. Tappert (Philadelphia: Fortress Press, 1959), 463–636.

4. Pelikan, *The Christian Tradition*, 4.

and aptitudes that might best be represented by the term "wisdom." Doctrinal statements, when they are doing their proper job in the activity of teaching within the community, function as instruments for the cultivation of wisdom.

Doctrinal statements have other jobs to do in other contexts. They often serve to represent, in an official or authoritative way, what the community holds to be true. They can be used in this way to teach those outside the community something about its central commitments. They can also function as reference points to settle questions within the community as to whether some belief or practice is in accord with the community's identity and mission. Each job may place its own requirements on the formulation of doctrinal statements. A statement that works well in the context of basic instruction within the community may not serve as well to represent the community's faith to the outside world, and vice versa. A statement designed with the precision and abstraction necessary to make it useful in settling issues arising within the community on certain points may be basically unintelligible both to the newcomer and to the interested outsider.

Doctrinal statements can and should take different forms for different purposes. This again indicates their instrumental character and suggests that a key question to be kept in mind in the formulation or reformulation of doctrine is whether the proposed statement is aptly formed to achieve its specific purposes. The "correctness" of a statement, in the sense of its agreement with what is taken to be normative in the tradition, may be a necessary condition of its success, but it is not a sufficient condition. There is a natural and necessary conservatism to the enterprise of doctrinal formulation, but unless the formulators also attend to the fact that doctrinal statements have specific functions to perform in specific situations, the statements will not realize their aims.

Considered under the heading of "teaching," doctrine has already revealed itself to be a complex phenomenon. Doctrine is the activity in which an understanding of a religious tradition is formed and guided. It is also the collective name for the statements—the "teachings"—that serve as the instruments through which that understanding is conveyed. Finally, it is that understanding itself: that which is really to be taught and learned through this process of instruction, by means of these instruments. One lesson to be learned through an apprehension of this complexity is that any approach to understanding Christian doctrine that restricts itself to the verbal formulations we often call "doctrines" without giving attention to the practices in which these are employed and the ends that they serve is not likely to produce an adequate account of doctrine.

Doctrine and Faith

In his very helpful philosophical study of religious doctrines, William A. Christian Sr. observes that the "primary doctrines" of a religious community—those that make up the bulk of its doctrinal material—will be "doctrines about the setting of human life and about the conduct of life in that setting."[5] The Christian doctrine of providence, if we may take the Heidelberg Catechism as illustrative of it at least to this extent, clearly fits that description: it is a doctrine about the setting of human life, and it either contains or implies some teaching about the conduct of life in that setting.

The notion of a (or the) doctrine "of" something—the doctrine "of providence," or "of creation," or "of the Trinity," say—can be traced far back in the Christian tradition but came into real prominence as teachers and scholars began to organize textbooks and presentations of doctrine according to specific topics, following the rhetorical strategies of their times. ("Topic" comes from the Greek *topos*, meaning "place"; the Latin equivalent is *locus*, which is why this way of organizing teaching, in its heyday when Latin was the language of scholarship, is frequently called the "*loci* method.") In each case, the topic was usually named for a leading concept having an important function in Christian teaching and Christian life. Thus, the concept of "creation" has been long recognized as a key concept in Christian understanding of "the setting of human life" (to use William Christian's phrase), and it is understandable that those bearing responsibility for the transmission of Christian teaching should have thought it

---

5. William A. Christian Sr., *Doctrines of Religious Communities: A Philosophical Study* (New Haven, CT: Yale University Press, 1988), 1.

worth a *locus* of its own, where it could be treated not in isolation from other concepts but with the depth and specificity it deserves. Schemes for organizing doctrinal topics into coherent presentations in textbooks and the like have varied from time to time and from writer to writer. Within these general schemes, the arrangement and relation of the individual *loci* can vary further. For instance, sometimes the doctrine of providence is located within the doctrine of creation; sometimes it forms a part of the doctrine of God; and sometimes it is treated as a separate topic. Each arrangement has its advantages and its liabilities. What concerns us at present is not the arrangement of doctrinal *loci* but their very reason for being. This long-standing practice of organizing Christian teachings around key concepts is an important clue to the function of those teachings.

Concepts—at least in the sense in which I am using the term here—are essentially *capacities*. To have been taught a concept and to have mastered it is to be capable of doing something one could not do (or, perhaps, could not do as readily or easily) before. The wisdom that comes with the absorption of Christian teaching is in large part the possession and deployment of a distinctive set of concepts. Those concepts form the understanding of self, world, and God that permits the practice of Christian life. They are close to the heart of what was once called "piety." (When I use the phrase "Christian understanding" in what follows, I intend it as a rough approximation to what "piety" once meant, before the modern debasement of the term. It refers more strictly to the cognitive element in that piety: to the "knowing"—not merely an intellectual knowing but an existential one as well—that helps to shape Christian being and doing.)

A Christian who lacks a significant Christian doctrine—let us say, the doctrine of creation—is therefore not simply *uninformed* about that point of Christian teaching. She or he is, in a way, *unformed* as a Christian, lacking in a range of conceptual abilities germane to Christian existence and practice. She or he does not know what it is to understand oneself as a creature of God, or to understand the other inhabitants of the environment as fellow creatures, or to understand God as creator. One might well take this to be a fairly serious gap in Christian understanding, with correspondingly serious consequences in practice. Having or lacking a doctrine of providence might be a similarly serious affair. One substantial clue to the meaning as well as to the importance of any doctrine can be found by asking what, if anything, this doctrine equips its holders to do: How do the concepts pertaining to this doctrine enable those who have learned it to apprehend things differently, to reflect differently on their experience, or to conduct their lives differently? What would be the consequences of the doctrine's disappearance from their lives?

Concepts are not the same as beliefs. It is often thought that the point of religious instruction is to furnish the learner with a stock of beliefs. Certainly coming to believe certain things—that is, coming to hold certain things to be true—is an indispensable part of appropriating a religious tradition. But when transmitting the right beliefs is taken to be the main aim of religious instruction, the believer may feel betrayed and helpless when, as sometimes happens, beliefs that were so carefully inculcated turn out to be inadequate, at least in the form in which they were received. (Indeed, the idea that there might be a distinction between the form and the substance of the beliefs, or between learning doctrinal statements and getting the point of the doctrine, may never have arisen.) In such a case, we might say that although in some sense—a deficient sense, we may think—the believer has been taught *what* to believe, he or she has not been taught *how* to believe.

Learning *how* to believe means learning how to use the concepts which are ingredient in our beliefs as instruments through which we may perceive, understand, and respond to our world. Sooner or later, this ordinarily comes to include learning how to revise our beliefs themselves, as our experience and the maturation of our faith may require. Faith involves a "propositional" element: it involves taking certain things to be true. But just what those propositions mean, and thus how they might be most adequately formulated to express their meaning, are points on which individual believers and their communities may well revise their judgments from time to time.

We speak of Christians and adherents of other faiths as people who believe the doctrines of their respective traditions. That is surely right. It might, however, be still more adequate to say that they believe *with* their doctrines. In the latter version, of course, "believe" is used in its fuller sense, to denote not mere assent but also the more existential dimension of faith. In the Christian community, doctrines achieve their proper function when the insights they carry and the concepts they contain help to enable that relationship of trust in and loyalty to God that "faith" in its complete sense normally conveys.

The believing associated with doctrine, then, is misunderstood if it is taken to be no more than a matter of believing the doctrines themselves. Doctrines help to shape a faith by providing concepts that give their adherents distinctive capacities for understanding "the setting of human life" and for conducting their lives accordingly. To believe a doctrine is more than to assent to its truth; it is to accept its resources for the shaping of one's understanding and thus one's faith.

Doctrine and Confession

The term *confession* may not have the meaning and resonance for all Christians that it typically has had in the Lutheran tradition to which we owe the phrase with which we are working ("We believe, teach, and confess . . ."), but for nearly all it will have some of the force pertinent to this discussion if we think of its use in the phrase "confessing the faith." To confess one's faith is to declare it or make it public. Christians have long recognized that this can be done in a variety of ways. The faith can be confessed by formulating and proclaiming a statement of faith—a confession or creed or doctrinal declaration. It is also confessed in the practice of Christian existence: one's faith is made manifest in one's actions.

What does doctrine have to do with confession? How is doctrine confessed? In the passage cited above, Pelikan associates the confession of doctrine primarily with the making of statements. It is "the testimony of the church, both against false teaching from within and against attacks from without, articulated in polemics and in apologetics, in creed and in dogma." There is no disputing that the verbal articulation of doctrine in forms such as those he mentions is one important way that doctrine is confessed. Further, his statement brings out a feature of confession that is rightly stressed in the Lutheran tradition: that confession or testimony is called forth most urgently at those points where the Christian faith and what it stands for are most at risk.

Just for this reason I would like to take the notion of the confession of doctrine further than he does in this passage. Doctrine is confessed whenever the wisdom informing Christian life is enacted—whenever, so to speak, we see that wisdom in operation. Specific doctrines—of creation, providence, grace, and so forth—are confessed in this sense whenever they make a manifest difference in the way their possessors sort things out, make decisions, and respond to their circumstances. That difference constitutes Christian witness. It may be direct or indirect, explicit or implicit, but in one way or another it bears a message about the God known in Jesus Christ. Even when it is most explicit and verbal, this witness may bear little resemblance to doctrinal formulation. Nevertheless, in it doctrine is being confessed.

In this respect, doctrines have a close association with virtues, as classically understood. A virtue (courage, for example) is a sort of aptitude: an ability to act in certain ways, together with a disposition to exercise that ability in the appropriate contexts. Courage manifests itself in courageous action. Doctrines, too, manifest themselves in conduct. At least they can do so when they have been genuinely learned and appropriated.

In short, doctrines make their presence felt not only—and not even primarily—where they are explicitly the subject of discussion. The force of doctrines comes in their confession: a confession that occasionally takes the form of direct doctrinal statement but is more commonly a matter of making the Christian witness manifest in appropriate words and actions, in the face of whatever threatens to obscure the truth it serves.

The "Christian" in "Christian Doctrine"

Doctrine, according to the foregoing account, may be best understood as a kind of wisdom. This wisdom can be formulated in doctrinal statements whose content and character may vary depending on the uses to which they are to be put (for example, instructing new members of the community, settling internal disputes over what should be taught, or giving an account of the community's faith to outsiders), and also depending on the contexts of those uses, that is, on cultural and historical circumstances. Doctrinal wisdom is enacted and made manifest, just as any other sort of wisdom is, when the community or its individual members draw on it in the decisions and actions of everyday life. To possess Christian understanding is to possess a distinctive sort of human understanding, a principal part of which is a distinctive repertory of conceptual capacities for apprehending and taking on the world.

What makes such understanding Christian? What makes doctrine or doctrines Christian doctrine or doctrines? Again, Pelikan's crisp definition can provide a place to begin.

First, he notes that Christian doctrine is "what the church of Jesus Christ believes, teaches, and confesses. . . ." In a broad, descriptive sense, Christian doctrine is whatever the Christian church holds and teaches as such. This seems self-evident. At this level, the only question one would have to resolve in determining whether a given statement was Christian doctrine would be whether one was entitled to say that the Christian church maintained it. The answer would depend in part on how one defined "Christian church" and in part on what counts as maintaining in this context. The fact that occasional Christians from time to time may have "believed, taught, and confessed" a certain point—say, the transmigration of souls— would hardly be enough to qualify that point as Christian doctrine, unless one were willing to grant that these Christians by themselves constitute the Christian church, so that whatever they hold and teach would be ipso facto Christian doctrine. Obviously, what would be sufficient evidence of churchly maintenance of a doctrine to qualify it as Christian doctrine is a matter for discussion. Should one follow the principle enunciated in the fifth century by Vincent of Lérins and restrict the title to what has been held "everywhere, always, and by all"? Would a consensus among major Christian branches be sufficient?

At this point the limits of a definition of Christian doctrine as "what the church teaches" become evident. It has its uses. But when questions or disputes arise as to what counts, normatively, as Christian doctrine—for example, as to whether the Heidelberg Catechism really represents the Christian doctrine of providence—another approach is necessary.

William A. Christian observes that, along with its "primary doctrines" about the setting and conduct of human life, a religious community is very likely to have what he calls "governing doctrines." These are "doctrines about doctrines," whose primary purpose is to deal with questions of this sort. Governing doctrines are addressed to questions such as (to use Christian's formula) "Is *s* a doctrine of *R*?"—"that is, questions which ask whether some sentence can be used to express, well and truly, an authentic doctrine of the community in question."[6]

Governing doctrines arise because the questions raised within a community about the authenticity of its own primary doctrines cannot be answered simply by appealing to the same primary doctrines themselves. Such questions "cannot be settled just by determining what members of the community have happened to believe or practice at some past time," nor "by polls to discover current opinions or by surveys of present practices of members of the community," since it is the authenticity of these very beliefs and practices that is at issue.[7] Some normative principles are needed.

This need for criteria is represented by another provision in Pelikan's definition: Christian doctrine is not merely "what the church of Jesus Christ . . . teaches"; it is "what the church of Jesus Christ . . . teaches . . . on the basis of the Word of God." We may take it that the latter phrase indicates, for Pelikan, the touchstone for determining whether something "believed, taught, and confessed" by the church—whatever the relevant sense of "church" may be— should count as Christian doctrine. What is meant by this criterion (that is, what is meant by "the Word of God" and how one determines whether something is based on it), as well as whether this is a correct and sufficient criterion for determining whether church teaching counts as Christian doctrine, are questions we may leave open for the present. The key point for our purpose here is simply that it is legitimate to ask whether a doctrine taught and held by a Christian community, and assumed by it to be valid Christian doctrine, really is a Christian doctrine.

---

6. Ibid., 1, 13.
7. Ibid., 16.

The Question of the Doctrine of Providence

In his autobiography, the philosopher and historian R. G. Colling-wood enunciated a basic principle of historical interpretation that has been put to use effectively in other contexts, including religious and theological discussion. He wrote,

> You cannot find out what a man means simply by studying his spoken or written statements. . . . In order to find out his meaning you must also know what the question was (a question in his own mind, and presumed by him to be in yours) to which the thing he has said or written was meant as an answer.[8]

This principle may be profitably applied, I believe, to some, if not to all, of the traditional doctrinal *loci*. Just as the topics generally took their names from concepts significant in their development, so they may be understood as attempts to answer specific questions. It makes sense to ask, then, of any "doctrine of" anything, What is the main question this doctrine was developed to answer?

The doctrine of creation, for example, might be approached as an extended answer to the question, How are we to understand the world theologically? The question itself has a different flavor in different contexts, and the contributions of various specific situations (e.g., the controversies over Gnosticism in the first two centuries of the church) to the doctrine are worth distinguishing and appreciating. The doctrine's very title, "creation," provides, in shorthand, the answer to the question: Understand the world as the creation of God. That title is also the leading concept whose unfolding constitutes doctrinal instruction and learning on this theme.

The question of the doctrine of providence might be formulated in this way: *How are we to understand theologically what goes on?*

Here too, the title of the doctrine provides a capsule answer and the leading concept through which the answer has traditionally been developed: Understand what goes on as the providence of God. The explication of that answer and of the concept of providence it employs may take considerable effort.

---

8. R. G. Collingwood, *An Autobiography* (London: Oxford University Press, 1939), 31.

Here, however, we are concerned not with the answer but with the question. The question itself calls for some explication, both as to what *sort* of understanding is sought and as to what the *subject matter* of that understanding is.[9] Let us take the subject matter first. According to the author of one of the twentieth century's few sustained treatises on providence, Karl Barth, "The doctrine of providence deals with the history of created being as such."[10] This represents as close to a consensus statement of the scope of the doctrine as one is likely to find in the tradition. One might say, simply, that the doctrine of providence deals with history. Many treatments of the theme in the last century take "history" as their central category, so that "theology of history" has in many respects replaced "providence" as a name for the topic.[11]

Given a sufficiently rich notion of what "history" encompasses, this would be a perfectly suitable designation for the subject matter of the doctrine. "History" would have to include not just human history but "natural history" as well, as Barth's phrase "created being as such" indicates. It would have to extend to questions now treated at the borders of scientific, philosophical, and theological cosmology, having to do with the history and destiny of the universe. It would have to encompass the "nonhuman" world (for lack of a better term): other living creatures and nonliving or inorganic substances (all of

---

9. Providence has played different roles in different theological accounts and systems. In the judgment of the contemporary Lutheran theologian Carl Heinz Ratschow, the differences among the major lines of development in Western Christianity (Thomistic, Lutheran, and Calvinist) have been so great as to render problematic the very notion of a coherent Christian doctrine of providence. (See his "Das Heilshandeln und das Welthandeln Gottes: Gedanken zur Lehrgestaltung des Providentia-Glaubens in der evangelischen Dogmatik," *Neue Zeitschrift für systematische Theologie* 1 [1959]: 25–80.) I would not claim that all writers on the doctrine of providence have been addressing the question I have identified as "the question of the doctrine of providence." I would claim, rather, that this question corresponds to the typical use of the doctrine and concept of providence in Christian understanding or piety throughout most of Christian history. More than a descriptive claim about what has been the case, however, mine is a constructive proposal as to how reflection on and reconstruction of the doctrine might usefully be organized.

10. Karl Barth, *Church Dogmatics*, III/3, trans. G. W. Bromiley and R. J. Ehrlich (Edinburgh: T. & T. Clark, 1960), 3.

11. As representative works in this genre, see Langdon Gilkey, *Reaping the Whirlwind: A Christian Interpretation of History* (New York: Seabury Press, 1976), and Peter C. Hodgson, *God in History: Shapes of Freedom* (Nashville: Abingdon Press, 1989).

these distinctions may prove to be quite problematic) on this planet and elsewhere.[12]

In the human realm, "history" would have to be understood as dealing not only with large collectivities of people, "world-historical" events, general movements and trends, and the like, but also with the most personal and subjective dimensions: with individuals' perceptions, feelings, personal relationships, decisions, and actions. Recall the personal tone and scope of the Heidelberg Catechism on this point, especially in its question 28 on the advantages of having a knowledge of God's providence.

Given such a rich and generous understanding of "history," the term would do. Unfortunately, the term has through long usage become associated almost exclusively with the human public sphere, so that either "natural history" or "personal history" sounds almost like a metaphor, an odd and somehow improper extension of the category. Moreover, we ordinarily think of history as the study of the human past (and of the human "historical" past at that, variously distinguished from the "prehistorical"). It takes a deliberate shift in our thought for us to apply "history" to the ongoing process or story, in its present and future as well as its past.

The less sophisticated, more informal, idiomatic expression "what goes on" thus seems to convey more readily what the scope of the doctrine of providence really is. It may be more useful precisely because it is a more colloquial term whose range is unspecified and because it is clearly not the property of any particular scholarly discipline or profession.

Now, as to the sort of understanding sought: What counts as a *theological* understanding of something? What is it to understand *theologically* what goes on?

Obviously, different kinds of understanding may be applicable to the same range of phenomena. The question "Why is this so?" for example, may admit not only of various answers but of various kinds of answers. The philosopher Alan Garfinkel's study of the nature of

---

12. If this seems too broad a scope for theological reflection on history, think of how often the vast size and age of the universe, or the mind-boggling complexity of life on earth, is invoked as evidence relevant to the question of the validity of traditional Christian notions of God's governance and care.

explanation opens with a familiar illustration of this point: "When Willie Sutton was in prison, a priest who was trying to reform him asked him why he robbed banks. 'Well,' Sutton replied, 'that's where the money is.'"[13] Sutton's reply was perfectly intelligible, and, given the question he assumed he was being asked, it provided a forthright and eminently satisfactory explanation for his actions. The point of the story hinges on our assumption that the priest was after another kind of understanding.

If we take "theology" in its broadest and most ordinary sense, to designate any talking or thinking about God, then we can say that to try to understand something theologically is to put it in the context of our talk or thought about God; it is to try to grasp it in its "God-relatedness." What does it have to do with God, and vice versa? What is the theological truth about it?

What this means more concretely will depend decisively on the inquirer's concept of God.[14] But it should be noted that one of the ways one's concept of God is ordinarily formed and developed is through trying to understand other things theologically. It is not the case that theological understanding is simply a matter of imposing a prior understanding of God on the data. There is a reciprocity to the process: one's understanding of God may be modified, more or less extensively, as one applies it to a theological understanding of the rest of reality.

A particular feature of theological understanding, at least given the sort of concept of God developed and deployed in the Christian tradition, is that it is always at the same time *self*-understanding, or "existential understanding," as it is sometimes called. God is always "the one with whom we have to do" (Heb. 4:13), in whatever we have

---

13. Alan Garfinkel, *Forms of Explanation: Rethinking the Questions in Social Theory* (New Haven, CT: Yale University Press, 1981), 21. Garfinkel goes on to discuss the "contrast spaces" assumed in any explanatory inquiry ("Why *x* rather than *y*?" Why banks rather than grocery stores? or Why rob banks rather than make an honest living?), which indicate what sort of explanation is being sought.

14. One of Karl Barth's complaints against many of the theologians of the post-Reformation period of Protestant orthodoxy was that their doctrine of providence showed scant evidence of having been affected by an understanding of the self-revelation of God in Jesus Christ. In his judgment, theirs was not a sufficiently Christian concept of God—at least when it came to this doctrine.

to do with anything else at all. To understand what God has to do with something is always at the same time to understand what it has to do with us, and thus to understand ourselves through it: it is to see it as something through which (to use the language of the tradition) God addresses us, and it is to understand how its God-relatedness is to qualify our own perceptions of it and our dealings with it.

Applied to the subject matter of the doctrine of providence, then, theological understanding asks, "What does God have to do with what is going on? What does what is going on have to do with God?" And to pursue these questions is at the same time to discover how what is going on impinges on our own self-understanding, and how, consequently, it makes a difference for our conduct.

In *The Responsible Self*, H. Richard Niebuhr wrote that, according to the ethics of responsibility he was developing in those pages, the question "What shall I do?" is always to be preceded by the question "What is going on?" One first attempts to discern what is happening; then one may determine what constitutes "the fitting response to what is happening."[15] In the version of the ethics of responsibility appropriate to monotheistic faith, he observed, the ultimately decisive element in what is going on is what God is doing in it: "Responsibility affirms: 'God is acting in all actions upon you. So respond to all actions upon you as to respond to his action.'"[16]

Niebuhr's ethics of responsibility is grounded in the doctrine of providence. Responsible action, on this view, depends on a person's possessing a theological understanding of what goes on that will equip her or him to discern the "God-relatedness" of each particular situation or incident and to make a fitting response. Questions such as "What is God doing?" or "How is God acting in this action on us?" are ways of specifying the inquiry that I have framed more generally as "How are we to understand theologically what goes on?" How best to specify the inquiry will depend in part on what ways of speaking about the God-relatedness of things one finds most adequate and least problematic. Should we speak of God's *action* in events? Or of God's

---

presence to the situation? Or is there another, more appropriate language for the circumstances? It will also depend in part on the sort of situation or range of data under consideration. The theological metaphor or analogy most suitable in one context may be less so in another. Niebuhr found that speaking of perceiving God's action in all the actions on us was highly useful in the realm of moral reflection. Others may have reason to prefer another idiom, in that realm or in others.

Theology and Doctrine

The question of the doctrine of providence—or, to be more explicit, the question to which the Christian doctrine of providence is addressed—is, How are we to understand theologically what goes on? The task of an exposition of the Christian doctrine of providence, then, is to set out the principles according to which, in light of the Christian witness, we are to understand theologically what goes on. How that task proceeds will depend in part on the intended audience and the intended use of the exposition.

This is—or at least, it can be—a *theological* task, in a more specialized sense of "theological" than the one employed previously in this chapter. In this specialized sense, the term *theology* designates a form of critical reflection *on* theology in the broader sense of our talking and thinking about God. Theological reflection occurs when we examine our talk and thought about God and ask ourselves about its validity. Christian doctrine, as one element of Christian talk and thought alongside others, is a fit subject for Christian theological reflection. Indeed, in view of the crucial role of doctrine in nurturing and guiding the Christian community and its members, and the authority that it is commonly accorded, it would seem that disciplined and rigorous reflection on its validity is especially important.[17]

Theological reflection on doctrine normally involves both a critical

---

17. Christian theology in this stricter sense might best be defined as critical inquiry into the validity of Christian witness. I have elaborated this definition into an account of the character of theological study in *Vision and Discernment: An Orientation in Theological Study* (Atlanta: Scholars Press, 1985).

assessment of existing doctrine and a constructive attempt to reformulate it insofar as the existing formulations are deemed insufficient. Such criticism and reformulation can be more or less radical. They can and should extend to the activities and aims as well as substance of doctrinal teaching, and they should treat doctrinal statements and formulations as the instruments they are.

One fairly significant example of the potential scope of doctrinal reformulation is provided by the proposal just outlined concerning the question of the doctrine of providence. The term and concept *providence* has traditionally come into play as Christian thinkers have formulated their *answers* to that question. It is nowhere required by the question itself. To put it bluntly: It is conceivable that what I have been calling "the question of the doctrine of providence" could be validly answered without making any use of the term or concept *providence*. It is conceivable that the time-honored use of *providence* in this connection has, all along, been a mistake; or that, although it was once an adequate concept to articulate a Christian response to this question, it is no longer.[18] Whether the term or the concept it represents should be retained in a contemporary reformulation of the doctrine is a matter for serious reflection. It may be that the question can no longer be answered by a doctrine of providence. On the other hand, it may be that what is needed is precisely a reinvestigation and restatement of what the providence of God, Christianly understood, involves.

There are theologians who question the value or even the justifiability of theological reflection on Christian doctrines. It is not that they believe doctrine to be beyond criticism; instead, they would prefer that the very idea of doctrine and doctrines be consigned to the past. In their view, a concern with doctrine distracts theologians from

---

18. Friedrich Schleiermacher represents the first view. In his major exposition of the Christian faith, he judges the traditional categories of the doctrine to be "nearly useless" (*ziemlich unbrauchbar*) and then goes on to note, "In any case, the term 'providence' is of foreign origin and was first taken over from heathen authors into later Jewish writings and adopted later by Church teachers, not without many disadvantages for the clear exposition of the authentic Christian faith" (Friedrich Schleiermacher, *The Christian Faith*, ed. H. R. Mackintosh and J. S. Stewart [New York: Harper & Row, 1963], 725). Karl Barth and Carl Heinz Ratschow, noting Adolf Hitler's habit of appealing to "Providence" as the divine justification for Nazi conquest, represent those who wonder—for various reasons—whether the term has been tainted by misuse beyond the point of possible rehabilitation. (See Barth, *Church Dogmatics*, III/3, 33, and Ratschow, "Das Heilshandeln und das Welthandeln Gottes," 25–26).

dealing with the pressing problems of the contemporary world. They would urge theologians to quit worrying about doctrinal formulations and start worrying about guiding their religious communities toward some resolution of the massive difficulties facing humankind: racism, economic injustice, the destruction of the environment, the resort to violence in conflict, and so forth. They view doctrinal theology as representing an intellectualistic misunderstanding of the character of faith and as something that tacitly if not explicitly encourages believers to be more concerned about the correctness of their beliefs than about the quality of their response to the world's suffering.

These charges are serious and embody a well-deserved critique of some perennial tendencies in theology and the church. But the proposed solution—the abandonment of doctrine and of critical and constructive reflection on it—is, to my mind, quite mistaken. If the account of the nature of doctrine I have sketched above is anywhere near the truth, Christian doctrine is not simply a collection of statements to be worked out, preserved, "believed," and handed on. It is more fundamentally the lived understanding of the faith possessed by the Christian community as a whole, by its constituent bodies (the various "churches" or denominations), and by its individual members. It is this lived understanding that informs and enables Christian practice, including faithful response to human need and to the issues confronting us all.

Doctrinal teachings function primarily to articulate, nourish, and discipline Christian understanding. To neglect them is not likely to make the Christian community any more responsive to the pressing issues of the day. Instead, it is likely to leave the community without an important means of cultivating the wisdom it has to bring to bear on those issues. And it is to leave the present understanding of the community—whatever its quality, sources, and results—to fend for itself, unexamined.

Over four decades ago, the British theologian G. F. Woods issued a call for "doctrinal criticism" as a distinct enterprise within theological study.[19] That call was not motivated by any desire to make

19. G. F. Woods, "Doctrinal Criticism," in *Prospect for Theology: Essays in Honour of H. H. Farmer,* ed. F. G. Healey (London: James Nisbet & Co., Ltd., 1967), 73–92.

theology less practical in its overall orientation. It was prompted by a sober recognition of the damage that unexamined doctrine can do and of the urgent need for doctrine that has been tested and refashioned to do precisely what doctrine is supposed to do: to furnish adequate guidance to and for Christian life.

The need for critical and constructive attention to Christian doctrine has not lessened in the intervening years, and it is nowhere more pressing, I believe, than in the case of the doctrine of providence. For some time now, the lived understanding of the Christian community has been malnourished when it comes to this doctrine. The basic affirmations of the Heidelberg Catechism regarding God's providence remain imbedded deep within the understanding of a great many Christians. At the same time, fundamental questions have, for many of those same Christians, rendered those affirmations so problematic as to leave them nearly useless. What sense might be given to the notion of God's "upholding" of "heaven and earth together with all creatures"? How, if at all, might the idea of God's "ruling" of everything that happens be made intelligible? Can we, and should we, understand unfruitful years, sickness, and poverty—or, for that matter, fruitful years, health, and riches—as in some sense provided us by God? Is the counsel of patience really the most pertinent advice Christians can give themselves and others when facing adversity?

On these and other points, there appears to be a profound dissonance between what the Heidelberg Catechism commends to us and what many of us find ourselves able to understand or willing to affirm. The result, in many cases, is a nonfunctioning or a dysfunctional doctrine of providence. The rudiments of the old doctrine remain, but they lack the sort of conceptual elaboration that would enable them genuinely to engage with contemporary sensibility and thus to function fittingly as instruments of Christian understanding.

Whether they can be given that sort of elaboration, or must rather be given up in favor of some more adequate basic orientation, is an open question. I am myself persuaded that there is sufficient promise in the concepts underlying the traditional affirmations to make the task of critical reappropriation and renovation worthwhile. At the same time, I am convinced that the result of such work will be, and should be, a doctrine of providence different in some important respects from what we have inherited.

Chapter 2

Providence Unfolded

*I*n the year 1694, William Sherlock, dean of St. Paul's Cathedral in London, published *A Discourse Concerning the Divine Providence*. It was one of several "practical discourses" through which this gifted preacher and writer was to have a pervasive and lasting influence upon the religious thought and life of English-speaking Christians, particularly in Britain and North America. There were other such treatises on the scene in the late seventeenth century, but perhaps none with its particular combination of conceptual clarity, scope, and accessibility. Sherlock's discourse on providence is one of the most lucid and comprehensive statements of the doctrine ever produced; although it is little known today, its influence continues to be felt. An examination of this work will provide a useful orientation in the doctrinal legacy with which we have to come to terms when we try to think afresh about the question of God's providence. In the next chapter, we will see how this understanding of providence attained the form and status it did, and consider what has become of it. Here, our objective is simply to gain a clear view of it.

Sherlock's avowed purpose in his discourse is both apologetic and pastoral. As a contemporary of Isaac Newton and John Locke, he was writing at a time when the doctrine of providence was just beginning to lose its hold on the Western consciousness and conscience. His aim, as he states it, is "so to explain the nature of Providence, as to reconcile men to the belief of it, and to possess them with a religious awe and reverence of the supreme and absolute Lord of the

21

world."[1] His discourse, then, is primarily a work of doctrinal exposition. It is not an exercise in natural or philosophical theology, in the mode that was already becoming popular in his day and that would come to dominate the early eighteenth century. It is a treatise in Christian doctrine, written with an eye toward the intellectual and practical problems being felt at the time. Sherlock is concerned to clear away "mistakes" about the doctrine that "tempt some men to deny a Providence, or so weaken the sense of it in others that they are very little the better for believing it" (9). The best way to accomplish this goal, in his view, was to explain what the content of the doctrine actually is.

The plan of his book is straightforward. There are nine chapters. The first, relatively brief, chapter—included only "that this work might not seem to want a foundation"—concerns "the proof of a Providence" (9), a subject he has in fact treated more extensively in his earlier *Practical Discourse Concerning a Future Judgment* (1692). Then the discourse proper gets underway. Chapters 2 and 3 are devoted to a careful explication of the basic concept of providence and of the key distinctions it involves. Chapters 4 through 8 then deal with various attributes of providence—its sovereignty, justice and righteousness, holiness, goodness, and wisdom. In these chapters he takes up the "mistakes" he mentions at the beginning of the treatise, identifying some common misapprehensions of Christian teaching on providence and answering the objections that stem from them. The ninth and final chapter concludes the discourse on a still more directly practical note, explaining "the duties we owe to Providence" (10).

---

1. William Sherlock, D.D., *A Discourse Concerning the Divine Providence*, 3rd American ed. (Nashville: E. Stevenson & F. A. Owen, Agents, for the Methodist Episcopal Church, South, 1856), 9. All seseqent citations of Sherlock's book will be from this edition, based on the third London edition (1702). A close comparison of the texts reveals that the differences among the first three London editions are extremely slight, and that the 1856 edition used here is essentially identical to the 1694 original except for the modernization of the typography—a change that commends this edition for our purposes here.

In quoting Sherlock I have preserved, without intratextual comment, his generally masculine language for both God and humanity, and I have allowed my own exposition largely to reflect his usage, in the belief that this does more justice to his perspective than would a more inclusive rendition. Coming to terms with this feature of his discourse and doctrine is part of the general task of critically appropriating this doctrinal heritage.

Now for some closer examination of the content of these chapters. The thesis of the first, "foundational" chapter is simply that belief in God entails belief in providence. The arguments—appealing both to pertinent biblical passages and to "the universal reason of mankind" (17)[2]—are mostly quite traditional, and Sherlock does not develop them here in any detail. His aim is simply to remind his readers of them. The arguments he favors, out of those he mentions, move from effect to cause and are aptly summarized in passages such as this one:

> This, I am sure, is very plain, that the same arguments which prove the being of a God, prove a Providence. If the beauty, variety, usefulness, and wise contrivance of the works of nature prove that the world was first made by a wise and powerful being; the continuance and preservation of all things, the regular motions of the heavens, the uniform productions of nature, prove the world is upheld, directed, and governed by the same omnipotent wisdom and counsel. (15–16)

Chapters 2 and 3 will require more extended treatment, for here Sherlock lays out the main conceptual distinctions he takes the Christian doctrine of providence to require. He begins his exposition of the concept of providence with a brief and compact definition:

> The general notion of Providence is God's care of all the creatures he has made, which must consist in preserving and upholding their beings and natures, and in such acts of government as the good order of the world and the happiness of mankind require; which divides Providence into preservation and government, which must

---

2. Scripture and reason are the two factors to which Sherlock consistently appeals in this discourse, as in most of his writings. There are occasional appeals to experience (e.g., "our own sense and experience," 155), and a very rare overt reference to the theological tradition (e.g., to Suárez, 23). This tradition has informed his thinking to a far greater extent than he explicitly acknowledges. In his strategy of arguing from Scripture and reason, Sherlock was quite representative of the Anglican theology of the Restoration period: appeals to experience smacked of Puritanism or "enthusiasm," and appeals to tradition or antiquity were associated with the scholasticism of an earlier day. The Bible itself was reasonable, and Sherlock, with his colleagues, took for granted the congruence of its deliverances with "universal reason" and their common power to overcome the mistakes brought about by undue reliance on tradition or religious experience. G. R. Cragg's *From Puritanism to the Age of Reason* (Cambridge: Cambridge University Press, 1950) is still a valuable study of this period; John Spurr's *The Restoration Church of England* (New Haven, CT: Yale University Press, 1991) may also be consulted.

be carefully distinguished in order to answer some great difficulties in Providence. (21)

Several elements of this definition call for comment.

First, in defining providence as God's care, Sherlock represents close to a consensus in the heritage of Protestant thought. The term *providence* (the Latin *providentia*, along with its Greek cousin *pronoia*) had been assimilated into Christian discourse from Greco-Roman religious and philosophical thought, but neither it nor any close cognate is much in evidence in the Bible. "The Lord will provide" ("*Deus providebit*" in the Vulgate) in Gen. 22:14 is commonly taken to be the single unambiguous scriptural precedent for the theological use of the term. Christian thinkers, aware of the mainly nonbiblical heritage and associations of the term, have generally been at some pains to specify the sense it should have in Christian usage and to distinguish that sense from other common alternatives.

This effort was especially important because *providence* can be taken more or less literally in some ways uncongenial to Christian understanding. On the one hand, it might be (and sometimes was) taken to mean simply "foresight" or "foreknowledge," God's foreseeing of what happens, in which case the affirmation of God's providence would amount merely to the assurance that God knows beforehand what is going to happen.[3] On the other hand, it might be (and sometimes, although more rarely, was) taken to mean "determination," God's "seeing to" whatever happens. In this case, to affirm God's providence is to say, in effect, that God has arranged beforehand to make whatever happens happen. Although some Christian thinkers were and are quite willing to affirm both of these statements—that God foresees and that God determines whatever goes on—neither of them has been generally thought to be an adequate rendition of the meaning of *providence* in Christian usage.

For Sherlock's contemporaries among Lutheran and Reformed theologians—the authors of the standard textbooks in what is com-

---

3. In some classical understandings of God's relation to time, it is not strictly accurate to say that God knows anything "beforehand": all times—past, present, and future—are immediately present to God, so God does not know things "in advance"; rather, God simply knows eternally what from a particular finite standpoint is yet to be. Whether such a concept of divine knowledge, with its related concepts of time and eternity, is coherent is another question.

monly referred to as the period of "high orthodoxy" in Protestant dogmatics—God's providence involves aspects of knowing, willing, and acting on God's part; but the definitions they offer usually focus on the acting as the distinctive factor in the concept. Providence is God's *opus* or *actio*, God's intentional work or activity.[4] And the character of this activity is, as Sherlock claimed, well represented as "care": a "looking to" or "looking after" or "looking out for" the creation, in general and in particular.[5] Sherlock's term, with its clear personal resonance, captures this character very effectively: providence is an active, personal relating.

This care is for "all the creatures [God] has made." The distinction and the relation between the activity of creation and the activity of providence are here affirmed. Sherlock was familiar with the conventional claim, found for example in many of the seventeenth-century Lutheran and Reformed theologians, that there are two "external works" of God, creation and providence.[6] Creation is the "work" whereby a reality other than God is established—a contingent reality, constantly dependent on God for its existence. Providence is the "work" that God does for and with that created world, given its existence. Sherlock accepted the logical distinction thus expressed, although he doubted that human beings are in a position to know whether the creation and the preservation of the world are two acts of God or only one (24–25).

---

4. "Providentia est opus dei unitrini externum, quo res a se conditas universas ac singulas potentissime conservat, inque earum actiones et effectus suavissime coinfluit, ac sapientissime omnia gubernat, ad nominis sui gloriam et universi huius atque piorum imprimis utilitatem," according to Johann Friedrich König, *Theologia Positiva Acroamatica* (1664, 1699) (from Carl Heinz Ratschow, *Lutherische Dogmatik zwischen Reformation und Aufklärung*, vol. 2 [Gütersloh: Gütersloher Verlagshaus Gerd Mohn, 1966], 210). Johann Andreas Quenstedt, who follows König's formulations closely, defines providence as "actio externa totius SS. Trinitatis, qua res a se conditas universas ac singulas tam quoad speciem, quam quoad individua potentissime conservat, inque earum actiones & effectus coinfluit, & libere ac sapienter omnia gubernat ad sui gloriam & universi hujus atque imprimis piorum utilitatem ac salutem" (*Theologia Didactico-Polemica*, 4th ed. [Wittenberg; 1701], 535). On the Reformed side, Johann Wollebius's popular *Compendium Theologiae Christianae* (1st ed., 1623) uses *opus* (see below).

5. The Heidelberg Catechism's rendering of the concept of *providentia* into German as *Fürsehung*, "seeing for," rather than the now more common *Vorsehung*, "seeing ahead," carries this connotation. A more recent writer has retrieved the use of *Fürsorge*, "caring for": Wolf Krötke, "Gottes Fürsorge für die Welt," *Theologische Literaturzeitung* 108 (1983): 242–52.

6. See, for example, Johannes Wollebius, *Compendium Theologiae Christianae* (London: T. Longman, 1760), 27; Quenstedt, *Theologia Didactico-Polemica*, 527.

This brings us to the first major distinction Sherlock observes within the concept of providence itself: the distinction between "preservation" and "governance." This is a very common division of the doctrine, antedating the Protestant Reformation considerably and frequently found in Protestant teaching. We encounter it already in the Heidelberg Catechism, where the equivalent terms are *upholding* and *directing*. Its popularity and its apparent naturalness may derive from the way it positions the doctrine of providence between the doctrines of creation and of the "last things" and refers it in both directions, so to speak. Preservation points toward the grounding of all things in God; governance points toward all things finding their end in God. Whether the context for such an understanding is provided by the relatively straightforward narrative structure of Christian Scripture and creed or by something like the *exitus-redditus* pattern of the neo-Platonic strand in Christian thought, we might say that with this basic distinction one of the fundamental ways the doctrine of providence operates in Christian life is to remind us that whatever is going on has both its ultimate ground and its ultimate goal in God.[7] Various New Testament passages anticipate this function in their own ways, placing creaturely life and creaturely events in the context of God's prior and subsequent reality: "For from him and through him and to him are all things" (Rom. 11:36) is perhaps the most explicit.[8] Just what this implies—that is, how this is supposed to inform Christian understanding and practice—is another question, to be addressed by a fuller treatment of the two sides of the distinction.

As he takes up the first component, the divine preservation, Sherlock takes his bearings from two other New Testament texts: "For in him [that is, in God] we live, and move, and have our being" (Acts 17:28 KJV), and "He [that is, Christ] uphold[s] all things by the word of his power" (Heb. 1:3 KJV). The contingency of creation means that

---

7. For a treatment of the interaction of these approaches in the thinking of Thomas Aquinas on providence, see Thomas S. Hibbs, *Dialectic and Narrative in Aquinas: An Interpretation of the Summa Contra Gentiles* (Notre Dame, IN: University of Notre Dame Press, 1995).

8. Ulrich Wilckens, among others, notes that a Stoic formulation—specifically, from Marcus Aurelius—seems to lie beneath the Pauline language here. Other somewhat similar ascriptive formulas are 1 Cor. 8:6, Eph. 4:6, and Heb. 2:10. Ulrich Wilckens, *Der Brief an die Römer*, vol. 2 (Zurich: Benziger Verlag; Neukirchen-Vluyn: Neukirchener Verlag, 1980), 272–74.

it needs the constant upholding power of God to remain in being: "God upholds all things in being from falling back into their first notion, and preserves their natural virtues, powers, and faculties, and enables them to act, and to attain the ends of their several natures" (22). A difference between God's creative activity and our own may be perceived here. The objects we make can, at least temporarily, remain in existence without a constant influx of power from us, because we are not responsible for the very existence of the materials out of which we have made them. We can destroy those objects by another exercise of our power, but we cannot actually *annihilate* them, that is, destroy the creaturely reality of which they are composed and thus render them nothing. God's creative activity, by contrast, must continue—not, Sherlock says, as a succession of re-creations, but as preservation, a constant provision of the power to be—if the creature is to continue in being. If God should will the non-being of the creature, this literal annihilation would not mean a further exercise of power on God's part, similar to creaturely acts of destruction, but rather only a withdrawal of the power that God gives the creature to be (23–24).[9]

In connection with the topic of preservation, Sherlock provides a brief treatment of the question of whether what he is calling preservation does not also include a second distinct providential act known in the traditional discussion as "co-operation" or "concourse." By the time of Sherlock's writing, a threefold distinction in the doctrine of providence—preservation, cooperation/concourse, and governance— was becoming standard in Protestant dogmatics. (Although Sherlock's Lutheran contemporary, J. A. Quenstedt in Wittenberg, is sometimes given credit for this scheme, it seems to have been introduced by J. F. König, from whose work Quenstedt liberally borrowed.) Sherlock acknowledges this tendency toward a further distinction but resists it. He grants, as part of the doctrine of the divine preservation, that "whatever we do we do by a natural power received

---

9. Sherlock allows that this will never occur: "There is one thing fit to be observed, that this act of preservation . . . is fixed by a perpetual and unchangeable decree; that though God will dissolve this present frame of things, and, it may be, cast the world into a new mould, yet nothing that is made, neither matter nor spirit, shall be annihilated or reduced into nothing again" (25).

from God" (25). But the doctrine of "co-operation or concourse" seems to imply that every act of ours requires a new, cooperating act on God's part; and if that is the case, what has become of our own natural powers? "If these natural powers, while they are preserved in their full force and vigour by God, can do nothing themselves without a new extrinsic determining motion from God, then they seem to be no natural powers, for they cannot act by nature if this be true. . . . This seems to make the world a mere apparition and empty show, which has nothing real" (26). The notion of "co-operation or concourse," which involves God directly in every creaturely action, seems to take away what the notion of preservation affirms: that creaturely reality has its own continuing integrity, thanks to God's upholding.

Sherlock allows that this is a difficult and subtle philosophical point, and he refrains from declaring the advocates of "co-operation" wrong; but he is clear as to what he does not want to give up:

> If we will attribute any thing to creatures, if we will allow that they ever act from a principle of nature, we must confess that God co-operates only to the natural power of action; that is, he only enables them to act according to their natures, without changing, influencing, determining their natures otherwise than these powers would naturally act. For this is all that is necessary to action when God has created the natural powers, and this is all the co-operation that can belong to God as the maker and preserver of all things. (26)

"Co-operation" or "concourse," then, in any legitimate sense, is simply a term for an aspect of the divine preservation, calling attention to the fact that we "move" as well as "live . . . and have our being" in God.

A further advantage to seeing "co-operation" as a part of preservation, in Sherlock's judgment, has to do with the question of God's responsibility for creatures' sinful actions. "Since no creature can move, or act, or do any thing, without the concourse and co-operation of God, some are wonderfully puzzled to give an account why God should co-operate with any creature in sinful actions" (29). If we understood God's "co-operation" as an immediate co-action with the creature in the sinful act, it would be difficult not to ascribe the sin to

God as well as to the creature.[10] But if, as Sherlock holds, God's involvement "comes to no more than God's preserving the natures of creatures, and actuating their natural powers to perform the offices of nature" (30), God is not the agent of sin. God is responsible, certainly, for making and preserving creatures who can and do sin. But that this makes God the author of sin is, to Sherlock's mind, "too absurd for any thinking man to say" (30–31). God deals with creaturely sin and its consequences in that aspect of providence that Sherlock calls the divine government, and it is there, rather than to the doctrine of the divine preservation, that we should look for further light on this question.

Sherlock's defense of creaturely integrity and freedom in connection with the doctrine of preservation may give the impression that he verges on Deism—an impression strengthened by his use of a familiar simile: This "natural co-operation of God can extend no farther than to the natural power of acting, not to any specifical acts. . . . It is only like winding up a clock, which puts it into motion, but gives no new preternatural motions to it, but leaves its motions to be guided by its own springs and wheels" (28). If so, the impression is dispelled early in his treatment of God's governing providence. Here Sherlock immediately affirms that "God is the supreme and sovereign Lord of the world, 'who doeth whatsoever pleaseth him both in heaven and in earth;' and therefore the absolute government of all things must be in his hands, or else something might be done which he would not have done" (36). Note the implication of that last clause: *nothing is done that God does not want done.* Sherlock is not content with an idea of "bare permission, as distinguished from an ordering and disposing Providence" (36). Nothing escapes the government of God. To show how God "orders and disposes," Sherlock makes several key distinctions within the divine governance. He begins with a distinction between God's government of causes and God's government of events.

---

10. Sherlock does not mention the common qualifications by which, for centuries, theologians had attempted to address this difficulty (see, e.g., Heinrich Schmid, *The Doctrinal Theology of the Evangelical Lutheran Church*, trans. Charles A. Hay and Henry E. Jacobs [Minneapolis: Augsburg Publishing House, 1959], 185–87); perhaps he did not find these efforts persuasive.

Sherlock divides causes into three groups: "natural causes," "accidental causes," and "moral causes" (also called "free agents").[11] With regard to the first, Sherlock affirms that "all natural causes are under the immediate and absolute government of Providence—that God keeps the springs of nature in his own hands, and turns them as he pleases" (39–40). In the natural world, things ordinarily "move and act by a necessity of nature," that is, according to the powers and laws God has bestowed on them. "God has bestowed different virtues and powers on natural causes, and in ordinary cases makes use of the powers of nature, and neither acts without them nor against the laws of nature. . . . God can temper, suspend, direct its influences without reversing the laws of nature" (37–38). This is not to say that God *cannot* act apart from or against these laws, but only that in the ordinary run of things it is sufficient for God's purposes to act within them.

The regularity of natural causes should not lead us to imagine that God is not involved in them. Everything that happens in the natural world happens because God directs it: the dependability of nature (the succession of the seasons, the properties and effects of fire and water, and so forth) and the specific things that happen within the natural order (droughts, bolts of lightning, and so forth), as well as the occasional exceptions to that dependability (miracles) are all God's doing. God "guides, exerts, or suspends the influences of nature with as great freedom as men act"; moreover, God's aim in so doing is often to govern human beings: rewarding or punishing, furthering or interfering with their plans (37).

Sherlock closes his remarks on this category of causes with some practical inferences: In the first place, we should respect God's governance of natural causes and learn to live within it. "We must not expect in ordinary cases that God should reverse the laws of nature for us" (40); rather, we should accommodate ourselves to this causal order as the context of our living. In the second place, we should understand how God is dealing with us through the government of the natural world, and respond accordingly. "All the kind influences of heaven which supply our wants . . . are owing to that good Providence

---

11. Again, he is drawing on the common doctrinal heritage in making these distinctions. Cf. Quenstedt, 553.

which commands nature to yield her increase; and those disorders of nature which afflict the world with famines, and pestilence and earthquakes, are the effects of God's anger and displeasure, and are ordered by him for the punishment of a wicked world" (40). God's government of natural causes has to do with the moral context as well as the physical context of our lives.

Given this understanding of God's direct control of all natural occurrences, it is no surprise to discover that the second category of causes turns out to be something of a mistake. There are no "accidental causes," strictly speaking. Nothing happens by chance. The category takes its life from our limited perception and from the great importance of apparent chance happenings in human life, rather than from a distinction in causes themselves. "What we call accidental causes, is rather such an accidental concurrence of different causes, as produces unexpected and undesigned effects; as when one man, by accident, loses a purse of gold, and another man walking in the fields, without any such expectation, by as great an accident finds it" (41). Though these "accidents" appear so to us, they are nevertheless the acts of God's governing providence.

> Upon what little unexpected things do the fortunes of men, of families, of whole kingdoms turn? And unless these little unexpected things are governed by God, some of the greatest changes in the world are exempted from his care and providence.
>
> This is reason enough to believe that if God governs the world, he governs chance and fortune; that the most unexpected events, how casual soever they appear to us, are foreseen and ordered by God. (42)

Passages from the Wisdom literature (e.g., Eccl. 9:11, Prov. 16:33), from the Pentateuch (Exod. 21:12–13, Deut. 19:4–5, the stories of Moses and Joseph), and elsewhere are cited in illustration and support of the claim, and Sherlock's treatment of the theme ends with some observations on the practical value of the doctrine of God's government of "what we call chance":

> This is the great security of our lives, amidst all the uncertainties of fortune, that chance itself cannot hurt us without a divine commission. . . .

> This is an undeniable reason for a perpetual awe and reverence
> of God, and an entire submission to him, and a devout acknowl-
> edgement of him in all our ways, that we have no security but in
> his Providence and protection. (47–48)

God controls the natural world, and natural causes are his own
instrumentalities. Furthermore, nothing happens by chance. Does
God then also control human action? How are we to understand
God's governance of the third category of causes—moral causes, or
(as Sherlock also calls them) free agents? Sherlock tells us that God
does use human beings as well as nonhuman creatures "as the instruments of Providence" (48), but he takes seriously the question of how
such use of human beings is compatible with human freedom. He
notes that many have denied their compatibility and have thus pitted
human liberty and providence against each other—a mistake he
wishes his readers to avoid.

To deal with this question, he introduces a further distinction, a distinction "between God's government of men, as reasonable creatures
and free agents, and his government of them as the instruments of
Providence" (49). In the former, which Sherlock calls "the government of grace," God's aim is the transformation of our sinful nature,
our forsaking sin and becoming virtuous. Our own responsible exercise of our moral freedom is indispensable in this process. Therefore
this aspect of God's government

> consists in giving him [that is, the human creature] laws, that he
> may know the difference between good and evil . . . and in annex-
> ing such rewards and punishments . . . as may reasonably invite him
> to obedience . . . ; and as this degenerate state requires, in laying
> such external restraints on him, and affording him such internal
> assistances of grace, as the divine wisdom sees proportioned to the
> weakness and corruption of human nature: and when this is done,
> it behooves God to leave him to his own choice, and to reward or
> punish him as he deserves; for a forced virtue deserves no reward,
> and a necessity of sinning will reasonably excuse from punish-
> ment. (49)

In the latter, though, which Sherlock at one point calls by the not
greatly illuminating name of "the government of Providence," the
focus is shifted. Here God deals with human beings not "in their own

private and natural capacity" as moral creatures, but rather "in relation to the rest of mankind" (49). Considering the effects of human beings' actions on others—the good or evil they produce in others' lives—"the Providence of God becomes concerned either to hinder, or to permit and order it, as may best serve the wise ends of government, as those other men who are like to be the better or worse for it, have deserved well or ill of God" (50).

According to Sherlock, in using us as the instruments of providence to others, God may, so to speak, temporarily suspend the government of grace and govern our "wills, passions, and counsels" more directly so as to bring us to do what he would have us do (51). Rather than (as in the government of grace) placing us in a situation of genuinely free choice, God will determine that choice by decisively influencing our minds in this instance. Left to ourselves, we might have done *x*; but God puts other thoughts into our heads—either gradually or suddenly, but in either case irresistibly—so that we change our minds and do *y*. "A man's heart deviseth his way; but the LORD directeth his steps" (Prov. 16:9 KJV): Sherlock finds ample testimony in Scripture to God's capacity to govern human action in this manner.

However, God need not always determine our decisions in order to make our actions serve the divine purpose. Such decisive control is exercised only "as often as he has any wise end to serve by it" (52), but obviously if God were to determine our wills constantly there would be no room for the government of grace, no opportunity for that genuine exercise of moral freedom that is essential to the renewal of our nature. God can govern our actions providentially without having determined the decisions leading to those actions:

> When God does not think fit to change and alter men's wills and passions, he can govern their actions and serve the ends of his providence by them. . . . The same action may serve very different ends; and therefore God and men have very different intentions in it. And what is ill done by men, and for a very ill end, may be ordered by God for wise and good purposes; nay, the ill ends which men designed may be disappointed, and the good which God intended by it have its effect. (54)

Good actions obviously serve the good ends of God, and their human agents are "the ministers of a good and beneficent Providence";

but God may also use "the ministries of bad men" (56). In doing so, God does not have any hand in their sins—"God never suggests any evil designs to men" (57), and so is not responsible for their corruption. God permits them to sin, and then directs the results appropriately, so that they produce unintended good. "If Providence consists in the care and government of mankind, how can God govern mankind better than to permit bad men to do no more hurt than what he can turn to good" (57). The wicked are commonly "the ministers and executioners of a divine vengeance upon each other, which is one great end God serves by the sins of men" (57). But there are other, more positive ends served by evil acts as well. Thus Joseph's brothers, meaning to do him harm, actually served God's purposes and were instruments of great good when they sold him into Egypt; thus the king of Assyria, setting out to destroy Israel, was actually God's agent for Israel's "correction" (55): "When God has no particular ends of Providence to serve by the lusts, and passions, and evil designs of men, he commonly disappoints them; . . . or he turns the evil upon their own heads . . . or he doubly disappoints their malice, not only by defeating the evil they intended, but by turning it to the great advantage of those it was intended against" (55–56).

So far Sherlock has been dealing with God's "government of causes"—the main subject of chapter 2 of his discourse. The government of causes has to do with how things come about, that is, with creatures' doings and with what God does by means of their doings. In chapter 3, he turns to the government of events. By "events," Sherlock means how things turn out, as distinct from what goes into how things turn out. Sherlock's basic claim here is that "the absolute government of all events" is in God's hands. Nothing whatsoever happens to any creature except that which God intends: "And indeed, were not this the case, Providence would be so insignificant a name that it would not be worth the while to dispute for or against it" (59).

Recall that Sherlock has taken steps both to secure the freedom of moral creatures to do good or evil and to remove God from any implication in the doing of evil. The divine concurrence ("co-operation or concourse") is to be understood simply as an aspect of the divine preservation, undergirding the natural capacity of creatures to act, rather than as a matter of God's coacting with the creatures in what they do for good or ill. The "government of grace" is a matter of restoring fallen human creatures to a situation of true freedom of choice so that they may (if they choose) obey God, acquire habits of virtue, and become fitted for everlasting life with God. In that situation of freedom, of course, they are and must be also free to disobey God and to subject themselves once again to the bondage of sin and its consequences. If they take this latter path, it is their own doing and not God's. When God is using moral creatures as instruments of providence, he may exercise a decisive influence on their wills (overriding their freedom, in a sense), but if he does so it will only be to influence them toward the good that they would not otherwise do; he will never incite them to evil. In Sherlock's view, human beings produce all the evil God will ever have a use for quite on their own, without any further inducement. God is never the agent or producer of evil. The most that can be said—and Sherlock is willing to say it—is that God permits creatures to do evil (e.g., 57).

When it comes to our suffering of evil, as distinct from our doing it, the idea of permission is not sufficient. God does not merely permit evil to befall us; he directs it upon us. God "orders and appoints what evils every man shall suffer," although "he orders and appoints no man to do the evil; he only permits some men to do mischief, and appoints who shall suffer by it. . . . And therefore we must necessarily distinguish between the evils men do and the evils they suffer. The first God permits and directs, the second he orders and appoints" (60–61).

But why should God direct evil upon human beings and appoint them to suffer it? For Sherlock, there is always a reason, and the reason may vary from case to case. The most common (though not the only) reasons have to do with "punishment" and "correction." On the whole, evil befalls people because they deserve it as punishment for their sin or because they need it as a discipline to turn them from sin, or both. Sherlock emphasizes the second of these and warns against a too-frequent resort to the first. It is obvious to him that in this life the virtuous generally suffer more evil than the wicked, so he is disinclined to interpret human suffering here and now primarily as punishment. His thinking is not that the virtuous do not deserve punishment; as all have sinned, there is none of us, even the most virtuous (Christ excepted), who does not deserve punishment. But Sherlock's overarching view of our life in this world is that it is a period of probation in which we are being shaped (or are shaping ourselves) for eternity. Rewards and punishments here and now—along with everything else that God sends us in this life—have, we might say, a more formative than summative aim. Eternal rewards or punishments will amply compensate for any disparity between what we deserve and what we experience in this life. (Sherlock elaborates this point later: "All the seeming irregularities of providence in this world, will be rectified in the next; and when we see this done, we shall then see the wisdom of what we now call the irregular and eccentric motions of providence. . . . For what difficulties are there, which eternal happiness and eternal misery will not answer?" [107].)

Our suffering in this life has, as a rule, a more immediate and practical purpose: to restrain us from sin (when illness or other affliction robs us of our resources, we have less opportunity to do evil) and to turn us toward God (when earthly pleasure and security are denied us, we may realize their limits and set our affections on heavenly things). The good things we are sent in this life likewise have a greater purpose—to encourage us in our struggles, to manifest God's goodness, or to enable us to do good to others—and we may be sure that at every point God sends us precisely what is right.[12] The evil that creatures do, then, along with the good that they do, God uses for his own good purposes: "In a word, God's government of all events is indeed so absolute and uncontrollable, that no good or evil can befall any man, but what God pleases, what he orders and appoints for him; and this is necessary to the good government of the world and the care of all his creatures" (66).

Sherlock's final point in his exposition of the concept of the divine government of events has to do with the distinction between general and particular providence.[13] He observes that some are willing to

---

12. Sherlock deals more fully with this matter in succeeding chapters; see, for example, 106–08. Susan E. Schreiner's *Where Shall Wisdom Be Found? Calvin's Exegesis of Job from Medieval and Modern Perspectives* (Chicago: University of Chicago Press, 1994) provides an illuminating account of the doctrinal tradition on the uses of affliction.

13. Some such distinction between God's care for the whole world (general providence) and God's care for each individual creature (particular providence) was common in the dogmatic tradition; it should not be confused with another common distinction (or set of distinctions)

grant that God exercises a general oversight of the workings of the world, but they deny that God is involved particularly in every event. They will affirm a general providence but deny a particular providence. Sherlock objects to this partly on logical grounds (e.g., the only way that God can take care of the world in general is to take care of every particular constituent of it), partly on scriptural grounds (e.g., Matt. 10:29–31), and partly on practical grounds (the importance to our faith of a confidence that absolutely everything that happens to us is according to God's will). He thus concludes,

> For if any good or evil can befall us without God's particular order and appointment, we have no reason to trust in God, who does not always take care of us; we have no reason to bear our sufferings patiently at God's hands, and in submission to his will; for we know not whether our sufferings be God's will or not: we have no reason to love and praise God for every blessing and deliverance we receive, because we know not whether it came from God; and it is to no purpose to pray to God for particular blessings, if he does not concern himself in particular events. But if we believe that God takes particular care of us all, and that no good or evil happens to us but as he pleases, all these acts of religious worship are both reasonable, necessary, and just. (69)

These two chapters give us the essentials of the Christian concept of providence as Sherlock understands it. The remainder of the treatise is chiefly concerned with elaborating the account of various aspects of the divine government so as to meet some common objections to belief in providence and to bring out more fully the practical consequences of the doctrine. My treatment of these remaining chapters will be selective rather than exhaustive and will aim at filling out the concept so as to offer a more detailed picture of the world Sherlock believed himself to inhabit.

Under the heading of "the sovereignty of providence," Sherlock takes up issues having to do with the "sovereign power" and "sovereign wisdom" of God—each an aspect of God's "sovereign will." In each case, he is attempting to resolve some misunderstandings. He

---

between "general" and "special," or even "general," "special," and "most special" providence, where the intent is to indicate that God's providential care takes different forms for different sorts or classes of creatures (e.g., for nonhumans, for humans, and for Christians).

affirms (with what he takes to be ample support in Scripture) that God's "power is absolute and his wisdom unsearchable" (70). God can do all things and does whatever he pleases (e.g., Dan. 4:35; Ps. 135:6); further, he "giveth not account of any of his matters" (Job 33:13 KJV): "How unsearchable *are* his judgments, and his ways past finding out!" (Rom. 11:33 KJV). Providence involves God's sovereign power and wisdom.

> But both these are thought very grievous by some men. They are terribly afraid of an absolute power which can do what it pleases, and justify whatever it does by an absolute and unaccountable will. Others are very uneasy that God does any thing without giving them the reason why he does it, and to be revenged of Providence, they will allow nothing to be wisely and justly done which they cannot comprehend. Every event which they cannot account for, they make an objection against Providence; and thus they may object themselves into atheism or infidelity; for they can never want such objections, while infinite and unsearchable wisdom governs the world. (71)

Sherlock's first step here is to clarify the concept of absolute power. The problem is that people imagine God's power on the model of "the arbitrary and tyrannical government of some absolute monarchs." The power of tyrants, however, is not true absolute power. Rather, "true absolute power can do no wrong, cannot injure and oppress its creatures; but will do good and judge righteously, defend the innocent, and punish the wicked" (71). Such is the testimony of Scripture concerning God's power (cf. Gen. 18:25), and furthermore it is "demonstrable *a priori*" on account of the unity of God's perfections: "absolute power can never be separated from absolute justice" (72). Injustice, Sherlock holds, is always the consequence of weakness, not of power (73–76).

In the course of his exposition of this point, Sherlock is led inevitably into the ancient question of whether God wills something because it is good or whether it is good because God wills it. He says that the question is ill posed, for it assumes "a distinction between the will of God, and justice and goodness, which in the divine nature are the same" (78). But since with our limited understanding we cannot grasp this unity, "it is more agreeable to the nature of things, to make good and evil antecedent to the will of God," so as not to give the impression that "justice and goodness have no stable nature of their own," or that God might make injustice justice simply by willing it (78–79). This resolution of the question turns out to have a practical point, for it enables Sherlock to oppose the doctrine of reprobation:

> There are a sort of Christians who attribute such things to God as are irreconcilable with all the notions we have of justice and goodness; and think to silence all objections, and to justify all, by the sovereign dominion and absolute power of God, which can do no wrong: but if it be a wrong to creatures to be eternally miserable for no other reason but for the will and pleasure of God, I cannot but think the absolute decrees of reprobation to be very unjust, and the execution of such decrees to be doing wrong, how absolute soever the power be that does it. (79)

Having thus established the trustworthiness of God's sovereign power, Sherlock might make short work of human grumblings about the inscrutability of the divine ways. Surely it is enough for us to know that whatever God does is right and "humbly to adore and reverence that wisdom which we cannot comprehend" (81), for "what greater security can creatures possibly have, that in the last great issue of things they shall suffer no wrong, than to know that they are under the care and government of infinite wisdom, that can do no wrong?" (82–83). But he realizes that this will not put an end to questions, so he develops an extensive account of the reasons for God's inscrutability. Along the way, he addresses several other pertinent issues. The main points, if not the arguments, can be briefly summarized.

Our incapacity as finite beings to understand the works of God is the first point Sherlock registers here: as God in effect told Job, those who cannot understand the making of a world can hardly be expected to understand the governing of it. Indeed, we understand ourselves and our fellow creatures so little that it is ludicrous to suppose that we could grasp an account of God's workings if it were presented to us. Whatever solutions are proposed to such philosophical questions as "necessity and fate, prescience and predetermination, and the liberty of human actions" seem to create intractable difficulties for the notion of providence, and it would be better just to leave all such speculation aside, as it oversteps the limits of our knowledge (86–88).

Another reason for the inscrutability of providence is that "the wise government of the world requires that the divine counsels, that the events and reasons of Providence should in a great measure be concealed from us" (90). If, for example, we knew exactly which of our sins were going to be immediately punished and which were going to be met with divine forbearance, we would very likely aim to avoid the former and indulge in the latter to the latest possible moment. Our ignorance of the future plays an important role in the moral development that is our task in this life. There is a dramatic, suspenseful character to human life in this world that depends on God's concealing things from us and then springing them on us: "The wise government of free agents, who so often change themselves, requires very frequent, sudden, surprising turns of providence" (92). In this connection, Sherlock develops further his understanding of the purpose of this present life: "If we must live in another world when we remove out of this, then this life is but one short scene of providence, and the government of mankind in this world is chiefly in order to the next" (107).

He also enters a warning here against prejudging the destiny in the next world of one's fellow creatures in this world, and particularly of those who have not had an opportunity to hear of Christ: "We know not what the condition of such men is in the other world, who lived in invincible ignorance of the true God, and of our Saviour Jesus Christ in this; this we confess we do not know, but believe so well of God, that we are verily persuaded, could we see what their state is in the other world, we should see no reason to quarrel with the justice or goodness of God on their account" (109–10).[14]

This leads him to a final point touching on the inscrutability of providence—a development, in a way, of his earlier objection to the "absolute decrees of reprobation." The notion that God created the great majority of human beings simply in order to make them miserable for eternity is not to be defended on the grounds that God's ways are past finding out. (Sherlock did in fact hold it to be "too certain,

---

14. This argument had already been developed at greater length in Sherlock's popular *Practical Discourse Concerning a Future Judgment* (London: W. Rogers, 1692).

that much the greatest part of mankind will be finally miserable" [115]; but it is because they misused their freedom and not because God has foreordained them to be damned.) It "must be laid down as a standing rule," he says, "that we must never attribute any thing to God, which contradicts the natural notions we have of justice and goodness" (116). This is, for Sherlock, not wishful thinking on our part but a rule God himself insists on (e.g., Ezek. 18, Jer. 12:1; 113). God's wisdom is unsearchable, but his will is always just and good: "Whatever we see done in the world, if it be possible to imagine any cases or circumstances wherein such a thing may be wisely and justly done, we have reason to believe that the infinite wisdom of God had wise and just reasons for doing it, though we know not what they are" (116–17). And if we cannot imagine any such circumstances, "is it not much more reasonable to suppose that we mistake the case, than to charge the divine providence with doing anything hard or unjust?" (117). This rule applies as well to God's "free and prerogative acts of goodness" in the economy of redemption, that is, to God's mysterious and gracious action on our behalf, preeminently in Jesus Christ. Rather than questioning God's goodness in waiting so long to send a savior or (to take the other side) questioning God's justice in sending one at all, we should simply acknowledge that God's grace, while it passes understanding, does not contradict God's goodness or justice but fulfills them (119–22).

A closer consideration of the justice and righteousness of providence in chapter 5 gives Sherlock opportunity to respond to further objections. He observes that people sometimes "impeach the Divine providence" for its apparent injustice: they note, first, that many people are unjustly deprived of their goods or are otherwise injured without just cause and, second, that "rewards and punishments are not justly and equally distributed; that some bad men are greatly rewarded, and some good men greatly punished" (123). The first point is a complaint against the *commutative* justice of providence ("giving every man what is his own by some natural or acquired rights"), and the second against its *distributive* justice ("rewarding or punishing men, as the nature and quality of their actions deserve") (123). Sherlock defends providence against each of these charges in turn.

First, as to commutative justice, he argues that the category simply does not apply here. We creatures have no rights in relation to God.

> God may very justly take away any man's estate, when no man can do it without injustice; and the case is the same with respect to honour and power, and life itself; for God is the supreme Lord and Proprietor of the world; we are all his, and all that we have is his; we have a right to our lives and liberties, estates, honours, and power, against all human claims; but we have no right against God; he may give riches, and honours, and power, to whom he pleases, and take them away again when he sees fit, without being chargeable with any injustice; for what he gives and what he takes away, are his own; and "may not he do what he will with his own?" (124–25)

"The justice of providence," he concludes, "does not relate to the rights of creatures, but to the moral and eternal reasons of things." This means that "though creatures have no natural rights against God, yet the justice and goodness of the Divine nature give them a moral right to such usage as they shall deserve" (125). We should confine our inquiry, then, to the question of distributive justice, and ask "what proportion there is between [human beings'] condition and their moral deserts; or whether they enjoy or suffer any thing which will not serve the wise and just ends of God's government" (126). The afflictions human beings are sent can in most cases rightly be understood as means of either punishment or correction, and thus as the proper consequences of sin. But the examples of Job, Joseph, Christ, and numerous others show that great sufferings may also be visited on human beings justly for good reasons other than punishment or correction (the overriding reason in Job's case was "to make him an eminent example of faith and patience" [129]). As long as they are amply compensated for their suffering in the long run, no "real injury" (128) has been done to the creature: "The sovereignty of God will justify the present sufferings of good men and prosperity of the wicked; and their final rewards and punishments will vindicate his justice" (131).

Why should not our actions receive their due immediately? Because

> this world is not the place of judgment, but a state of trial, probation, and discipline, where good men many times suffer, not so

much in punishment of their sins, as to exercise their faith and patience, and to brighten their virtues, and to prepare them for greater rewards; and bad men are prosperous, to lead them to repentance, or to make them instruments of the Divine providence in chastising the wickedness of other men, or the more remarkable examples of the Divine justice and vengeance in their final ruin. (132)

Although the delay of divine justice is itself a great trial to the righteous (as the Psalms often testify), it serves God's purposes without fail, and we should make use of it accordingly.

The aim of the divine government is a theme Sherlock continues to pursue when he takes up the subject of the holiness of providence. His concern here is to show "how the external administrations of providence encourage virtue, and discourage wickedness and vice" (145). The fact that God permits sin is no argument against the holiness of providence; it is entirely consistent with it. God could not prevent sin without preventing liberty, and this would eliminate the moral good that is holiness in the creaturely realm. "Does government signify destroying the nature of those creatures which are to be governed? Does this become God, to make a free agent, and to govern him by necessity and force?" (150). God does govern our minds, but (as Sherlock has already told us) in a manner appropriate to our moral nature. That government consists in doing everything possible to encourage us toward right choices and to discourage us from evil, while preserving our liberty. God may sometimes override that liberty and direct our decisions for the good of our fellow creatures, but if we are to become holy he must ordinarily not interfere with our liberty but must instead permit and enable its full exercise. At the same time, God may and does prevent the actual commission of a great deal of the wickedness human beings are resolved to commit by hindering them in carrying it out, and the evil that is actually carried out, God directs upon those who need or deserve it. Thus the liberty of inward choice requisite to holiness is preserved, and no more actual evil is produced through the carrying out of evil choices than will serve God's purposes: "Considering the great wickedness and degeneracy of mankind, we have reason to believe that God hinders a hundred times more than he permits" (155).

In this context Sherlock reiterates the principle that God is not the author of evil. God never coerces, incites, or encourages anyone toward an evil choice or its execution, for this would be inconsistent with God's own holiness and goodness, as both Scripture and reason conclusively demonstrate (155–57). God foreknows our choices and their possible consequences, and arranges things so that the actual consequences of those choices accomplish his will. Sherlock offers an interpretation of Acts 2:23 ("Him, being delivered by the determinate counsel and foreknowledge of God, ye have taken and by wicked hands have crucified and slain" [KJV]) in exemplification of this point: God determined that Christ should die but did not induce his killers to kill him. Rather, "by his infinite prescience and foreknowledge he saw by what means this would be done, if he thought fit to permit it" (161), and so it was accomplished—the guilt accruing to the slayers, and the praise to God.[15]

A number of other biblical texts that appear to attribute evil to God receive Sherlock's scrutiny in the remainder of chapter 6. For example, God's hardening of Pharoah's heart (Exod. 4:21) was not, as Sherlock reads it, a matter of God's "infusing" hardness into it. Pharoah had already hardened his own heart through a succession of evil choices. God knew that Pharoah would abuse every opportunity for repentance, no matter how winsomely presented, and was "ripe for destruction"; God determined therefore to offer him such circumstances as would allow him to confirm himself in that evil character (circumstances that would in themselves tend to soften the heart of anyone less thoroughly committed to unrighteousness), so that he might become an "infamous example of wickedness" and "deserve a more glorious and exemplary vengeance" (165). Other cases of "hardening" and other texts in which God appears to be responsible for the evil that is done (and responsible thus for the eter-

---

15. That the Jewish people bear the guilt for Jesus' death—the Roman officials being only their accessories—and that their subsequent miseries (from the destruction of Jerusalem onward) are God's just judgment upon them for this crime, are claims Sherlock not only takes for granted but argues explicitly (cf. 169–70, 283–84). Although they have been repudiated officially by some major Christian bodies in the wake of the Holocaust, they are still accepted by large numbers of Christians and are reinforced in countless sermons. This is, to say the least, one of the most harmful aspects of this doctrinal legacy.

nal misery of the creaturely doers of it) are dealt with along the same lines: as instances in which God, knowing that the individuals concerned are determined to follow an evil course, leaves them to it and makes the result serve a good and holy end. "To say that God decrees the sins of men for his own glory, to magnify his mercy and justice, in saving some few, and in condemning the greatest part of mankind to eternal miseries, is so senseless a representation both of the glory, of the mercy, and of the justice of God, as destroys the very notion of all" (185).

Sherlock concludes chapter 6 with a moral inference: "The holiness of providence teacheth us never to do any evil to serve providence, under pretext of doing some great good by it, which we think may be acceptable to God" (186). Although God brings good out of evil, we are never justified in doing evil on account of the good we believe it may lead to. "It is certain a wise and holy God requires no such thing of us" (186); on the contrary, God requires us to do the good even when it seems clear to us that some evil action would in the long run be productive of more good: "Let us lay down this as a certain principle, that God needs not our sins; and that we can never please him by doing evil, whatever the event be; he makes use of the sins of men to serve his providence, but he will punish them for their sins" (187).[16]

The next attribute of providence Sherlock considers is its goodness. This is, he says, "a more proper subject for our devout meditations than for our inquiries" (187), since evidence of the abundance of God's goodness is all around us. Indeed, "atheism is founded in ingratitude" (188). But that ingratitude itself may rest on certain mistakes in thinking that render one incapable of seeing the goodness of providence, and so Sherlock addresses those mistakes and the attendant objections.

---

16. In this rejection of "consequentialist" ethics, Sherlock has a great deal of company among writers on providence: for example, his older contemporary John Wilkins (*A Discourse Concerning the Beauty of Providence* [6th ed., London: 1680]) and in our own time the Lutheran theological ethicist Gilbert Meilaender (*The Limits of Love* [University Park, PA: Pennsylvania State University Press, 1987], 63–67 and 83–84). Meilaender observes that consequentialist ethics could make serious inroads in Christian ethical thought only after the classical Christian vision of God's governing providence had faded.

The first mistake consists in an inclination to think of God's goodness in the abstract, "without relation to the nature, quality, or desert of the subjects who are to receive good" (189–90). The original state of creation shows what God's goodness can achieve, but that is not the state in which we live. Human sin has transformed our circumstances, and now, "the degenerate state of mankind requires such a mixture of good and evil as we now see, and feel, and complain of in this world" (191). We are in "a state of trial and discipline" (192) and should expect no more of God's goodness and justice than what such a state will allow:

> A state of discipline must neither be a state of perfect happiness, nor misery, but an interchangeable scene of very agreeable pleasures and tolerable evils, sufficient to exercise the virtues, and to correct the vices of mankind: and this I take the state of this life to be; so happy, that few men are so miserable as to be weary of it; and yet so intermixed with troubles, as to exercise the virtues of good men, and to correct the wicked: and this is what becomes the goodness of God to do for us in a state of discipline. (194)

Although the wicked may sometimes thrive and the good be afflicted during this earthly life, on the whole God makes plain the consequences of virtue and vice, sending contentment to the good and visiting the results of evildoers' sins upon themselves here and now, as well as hereafter (194–95). Evil will never be allowed to overwhelm the good. "Good men must suffer no more than what will increase their virtue, not prove a temptation to sin. . . . The sufferings of bad men, who are in a curable state, must be only proportioned to their cure, unless the evil of the example requires a severer punishment to warn other sinners" (196). God is patient and long-suffering, dealing kindly with sinners, sending sunshine and rain upon both the just and the unjust, and in general providing far more good to this world than it deserves: "The evils that are in the world bear no proportion at all to the good: there are some few examples of miserable people, but the generality of mankind are very happy; and even these miserable people have great allays of their miseries, and if we take an estimate of their whole lives, have a much greater share of good than evil" (197).

A further mistake consists in overlooking the distinction between "the good of the end and the good of the means[:] The end is happiness, which is the good of nature . . . ; the good of the means is that which is good to make men happy" (198). Sherlock continues by arguing that "we can neither prove nor disprove the goodness of providence merely by external events, especially with respect to particular men. For prosperity is not always good for us, nor is affliction always for our hurt" (199).

Another mistake with regard to God's goodness in providence is to overlook the fact that God must attend to "the good of the whole" and not only to each particular creature (204). What happens to individual creatures sometimes has a greater purpose than that particular creature's needs or deserts in view. Thus, an impressive calamity— the destruction of an evil city by fire or flood, say—may be brought about to serve as a terrifying example of God's judgment. If so, we may be assured by the principles Sherlock has already enunciated that no inhabitant of that city receives any injustice at God's hand; but by this event, many others receive warning and are brought to repentance and amendment of life.

Once these mistakes are corrected, we may see that the miseries of this life are no objection to the goodness of providence. Creatures must be given the freedom that allows them to commit sin if they are to realize their nature and destiny in holiness and happiness; creatures who use that freedom to commit sin must be disciplined for their own sake and sometimes punished as an example to others. No one may justly blame God for dealing with us as we deserve. On the contrary, we should be grateful for God's continuing patience and forbearance and kindness in making this world "so tolerable a place" (226), for sending us far fewer evils and far more good things than we deserve, and for making our lives generally pleasant in the midst of our troubles.

> It is not always in our power to avoid many of the sufferings and calamities of life, but it is our own fault if we sink under them. Natural courage and strength of mind, the powers of reason, and a wise consideration of the nature of things, the belief of a good providence, which takes care of us, and orders all things for our good, and the certain hope of immortal life,—will support good men under their sufferings, and make them light and easy. . . . What is merely external, may afflict a good man, but cannot make him

miserable; for no man is miserable, whose mind is easy and cheerful, full of great hopes, and supported with divine joys. . . .
. . . [A]nd if we be not thus happy under all our sufferings, it is our own fault. (229–30)

The wisdom of providence is the final attribute Sherlock considers. Though the "unsearchability" of the wisdom of God (previously discussed under the rubric of the sovereignty of providence) should keep us from judging what we cannot comprehend in God's dealings with the world, "it becomes us to take notice of, and to admire that wonderful wisdom which is visible in the government of mankind" (233). Sherlock proposes here first to examine certain "hinges of providence" as recorded in the scriptural account of human history, and then to consider "some other visible marks and characters of wisdom in the more common events of providence" (234) in ordinary experience. For the first, he offers a brief rehearsal of the scriptural narrative from the creation onward to the first century of the Christian era, showing at key points why things went as they did and what wisdom God displayed in giving events this turn. We need not pursue this particular account in any detail, except to note that it involves an interpretation of the relation of Judaism to Christianity that is quite common in the Christian tradition:

God had accomplished what he intended by the carnal posterity of Abraham; that is, he had preserved and propagated the knowledge of the one true God in the world, and prepared men to receive Christ when he should be preached to them; and now Christ was come, the spiritual covenant took place, which was not confined to Abraham's carnal posterity, but extended to all that believed in Christ all the world over. So that God had no longer any one nation for his peculiar people; but those only were his peculiar people, whatever nation they were of, who believed in Jesus.

The Jews, then, considered as Abraham's carnal posterity, were God's peculiar people no longer; nor did God's promise oblige him to preserve them a distinct nation any longer; and therefore the Divine providence might now as justly destroy them as any other nation, if they deserved it, and certainly the crucifixion of their Messias, and their obstinate infidelity, did deserve it. And when they had thus justly deserved a final excision, the Divine wisdom had admirable ends to serve by it. (283–84)

As for the evidence of the wisdom of providence in events beyond Scripture, Sherlock confines himself to a few common instances. He begins by observing the way "God rewards and punishes men in their posterity" (286), which is to say that the children of the wicked are often still more wicked (and thus more deserving of punishment) themselves, while the children of the righteous generally continue in righteousness and in the rewards thereof.

> All good men are not prosperous in this world, nor has God any-where promised that they shall be so, no more than all wicked men are visibly punished here; but as God visits the iniquities of the fathers upon their children, by executing a more speedy vengeance on the wicked children of wicked parents; so the righteous children of righteous parents shall be more certainly prosperous than other good men; and the more uninterrupted successions there are of such righteous parents and righteous children, the deeper root they shall take. (289)

This consideration should lead parents to seek righteousness for their children's sake as well as for their own, and it should lead children to "avoid the evil examples and to imitate the virtues of their parents" (290). The implications for societies and nations are not far to seek, either.

Sherlock moves on to observe how often sin is punished with like sin ("oppression is often punished with oppression, adultery with adultery, murder with murder, and wicked men are made plagues and scourges to each other" [292])—a pattern that serves to show vividly the evil of sin. He instances the fact that God "so often disappoint[s] both our hopes and fears" (292) as evidence of God's wisdom in leading us to trust in God alone. And he suggests that this wisdom is further displayed in God's sometimes reducing a people to extremities in order to turn them to God, in the sudden and unpredictable changes of social and political fortune that make it impossible for people to act "by a politic foresight of events" (294) and in "the wise mixture and temperament of mercy and judgment" (295) in God's dealings. In all this, as in much of what Sherlock has to say about the ways of providence generally, the experience of the English church and people earlier in his century may not have been far from his mind.

The final chapter of his discourse concerns "the duties which we owe to providence" (296). He has, of course, drawn some practical inferences for conduct as he went along, but now he turns more directly and extensively to the question. He summarizes four major duties. The first is "[t]o take notice of the hand of God in every thing that befalls us; to attribute all the evils we suffer, and all the good things we enjoy, to his sovereign will and appointment. This is the foundation of all the other duties which we owe to providence, and the general neglect of this makes us defective in all the rest" (296). The foundational character of this duty is plain enough: if we are to respond to God's providence, to live according to it, we must first understand our lives by it. We must learn the habit of interpreting everything that happens in the light of this, so that we "receive all as from the hand of God" and "live under a constant sense and regard" of God's working in all things (297).

The next duty is "to compose our souls to a quiet and humble submission to the sovereign will and pleasure of God in all things" (298). To recognize God's providence is one thing; to submit ourselves to it is another. The nature of this submission Sherlock articulates in several points. Submitting to providence when it brings affliction is, obviously, a more difficult task than submitting to the good we receive at God's hand, so Sherlock offers some guidance on this head. Submission "does not require that we should not feel our sufferings" or that we should cease to bear them in distinctively human ways, "with pain, and grief, and reluctancy, with sighs, and groans and complaints, with vehement and importunate desires and prayers to God and man to help and deliver us" (299). The Psalms, and Christ's own example, teach us this. In our complaining, however, we are not to reproach God. "Now a man who suffers with submission, must not reproach and censure the Divine providence, but think and speak honourably of God, how hardly soever he deals with him; he may complain of what he suffers both to God and men, but he must not complain of God" (300). We must wait patiently for God's deliverance, thinking of God as "the universal Parent, who has a tender and compassionate regard for all his creatures. . . . When we know that it is a kind hand which strikes, we shall kiss the rod and submit to correction with as equal a mind, as we do the prescription of a physician, how severe soever the methods of cure are" (302).

Submission to God's providence also requires us to give due attention to "the several states, conditions, and relations of life, which the Divine providence hath placed us in" (303). We are faithfully to discharge the duties belonging to our station in life, whatever it may be. God has ordained inequalities of station as necessary for good government and social order as well as for the overarching purposes of providence itself (cf. 230–33). We may rightly strive to improve our situation with honest, responsible, and patient effort, but we must not chafe against what God has given us nor "force ourselves upwards" out of our place (307). "Submission to providence requires us quietly and contentedly to keep our station till God sees fit to advance us, at his own time, and in his own way" (308). If God sees fit to elevate (or lower) us to a different station in society, we must accommodate ourselves then to that situation and its duties.

Submission to providence does not, however, require us passively to acquiesce to whatever anyone wishes to do to us, says Sherlock, citing the following example: "If a thief breaks open my house, or robs me upon the road, submission to providence does not hinder me from pursuing and taking him, and recovering my own of him, and bringing him to punishment, if I can; for my being robbed lays no obligation upon me patiently to lose whatever is unjustly taken away, if I have any honest way left of recovering it" (310). The same is true in the case of an intended conquest by foreign enemies or under the threat of a natural disaster. In all such cases, we are entitled, even obliged, to defend ourselves and what is entrusted to us by all lawful means. It is only when the deed is done that we are to understand it as God's will for us—not in advance, or while the outcome is still at issue.

Submission to providence does not require, finally, that we excuse the human agents who are "causes and instruments" of our sufferings. Even though it is God who has brought the evil they have done upon us, their doing of it is still sinful, and they are accountable for it. However, "submission to providence will greatly mitigate our resentments, and calm our passions, and keep them within the bounds of reason and religion" (311). We are to be angry not at what they have done to us (for this was indeed God's will) but at their wickedness in doing it; and we are to deal with them as God would have us deal with them, and not as our self-love and our sense of injury would dictate.

Along with submission, another duty we owe to providence is "an entire trust and dependence on God" (312–13). If submission has to do with what has already befallen us, trust and dependence (or, as Sherlock also puts it, "faith, and hope, and trust") is oriented toward the future. But what does this amount to? What are we to trust God for, and how far are we to trust? We must certainly not trust that God will do whatever we wish to have done. "Has God anywhere promised to give us whatever we trust in him for?" (313). Rather, we must trust God to do what God has promised to do, and we must be careful not to interpret those promises rashly. God has made promises "to states and kingdoms," as well as to human beings "in their private and single capacities," and if we understand these promises we will understand in what a proper trust in God's providence consists (314).

God's promises to "states and kingdoms" are an extension of God's promises to "the Jewish church and nation," according to Sherlock: "When a nation has embraced Christianity, and the church is incorporated into the state, and true religion and virtue are encouraged, and vice suppressed, such a religious nation has a title to all the national blessings which God promised to the Jewish nation, if they observed his laws" (314–15). These blessings are both spiritual—an increase of virtue and its enjoyment—and temporal: "God has oftentimes suffered a wicked nation to be prosperous to scourge their wicked neighbours, but he never suffers a truly righteous and religious nation to be oppressed" (315).

The promises to "good men" in their private capacity are of a different order. God promises "that he will always take care of them as a father takes care of his children" (317), but this obviously does not mean a guarantee of temporal prosperity or of freedom from oppression. It does, however, mean that they will ordinarily receive the food and raiment necessary to sustain life (although this too may be lacking in extraordinary circumstances), and, more importantly, it means that "all things shall work together for good" to them, so long as they continue in faith and hope (318). They may be sure that in all things

God will do what is for their good, however different this may be from what they imagine.

The final duty Sherlock mentions is prayer, chiefly petitionary prayer, "to ask of God all those blessings and mercies which we need" (323). Though God certainly knows what we need before we ask it, he has also often expressly made our asking the condition of our receiving it (325): "Parents expect this of their children, and a prince from his subjects, and will see their wants, and let them want on till they think fit to ask: and if wise and good men expect this from their dependents, a wise and good God may as reasonably expect this from his creatures" (326–27). We do not pray, then, to inform God of our needs, nor to make ourselves aware of our dependence, but to acknowledge that dependence as we should. And it is not inappropriate to think of God as being moved by our prayers, inasmuch as Scripture itself attributes affections to God and offers instances of this sort (329). For similar reasons, "praise and thanksgiving are as essential a part of the divine worship, and as much due to God's care and providence over us, as prayer is" (332). Moreover, praise and thanksgiving become us: "To contemplate and adore the Divine wisdom and goodness which encompasses the whole creation, and dispenses his favours with a liberal hand, is a more transporting pleasure than all the enjoyments of the world can give us. Here is a noble exercise of love, and joy, and admiration, which are the most delightful passions of the soul" (333). The sense of providence, exercised in praise and thanksgiving, is the key to our own happiness.

"And thus," Sherlock concludes, "I have finished this discourse of providence; whereby I hope it will appear, that there are great reasons to believe a providence, that the objections against it are ignorant mistakes, and that nothing tends so much to the ease, and comfort, and good government of our lives, as to acknowledge God to be the supreme sovereign Lord of the world" (336). At the very least, Sherlock has given us a view into the world as he conceived it theologically and a valuable account, from a reflective participant's standpoint, of the doctrinal heritage with which we must come to terms.

Chapter 3

The Scope of Providence

> *"We mustn't question the ways of Providence," said the Rector.*
> *"Providence?" said the old woman. "Don't yew talk to*
> *me about Providence. I've had enough of Providence. First*
> *he took my husband, and then he took my 'taters, but there's*
> *One above as'll teach him to mend his manners, if he don't*
> *look out."*
> *The Rector was too much distressed to challenge this*
> *remarkable piece of theology.*
> *"We can but trust in God, Mrs. Giddings," he said.*
> *—Dorothy L. Sayers,* The Nine Tailors[1]

A Problematic Legacy

Here is an entry from the diary of Thomas O. Summers (1812–1882), an English immigrant to America who became one of the leading theologians of the Methodist Episcopal Church, South, and founding head of its publishing house:

> Nashville, February 15, 1872.—On going to the Publishing House this morning I found my office, library, papers, etc., in ashes. About midnight a fire broke out in the bindery, and burned it, my office, the composition and stereotype rooms. My journal, which I had

---

1. Dorothy L. Sayers, *The Nine Tailors* (San Diego, CA: Harcourt Brace Jovanovich, 1962), 68.

kept for forty years, manuscript works on Retribution, Hymnology, the Church, notes on Scripture, sermons, commonplace-books, autograph letters of the Wesleys, Coke, Asbury, Watson, and other distinguished men, and my library worth thousands of dollars, were all consumed.

Summers concluded the entry thus:

The Lord would not have permitted so great a calamity to happen to me, if he had not intended to overrule it for good; so I submit without murmuring. I take out a new lease of life, and begin the world anew; yet I feel the stroke so keenly.[2]

About two decades before this event, Summers had seen through the press the third American edition of William Sherlock's *Discourse Concerning the Divine Providence.* His diary entry testifies to the continuing force of the understanding of providence Sherlock's book represents. Sherlock's book, first published in London in 1694, was the last of a group of influential seventeenth-century treatises on providence—including John Wilkins's *A Discourse Concerning the Beauty of Providence* (1649), Thomas Crane's *Prospect of Providence* (1672), and John Flavel's *Divine Conduct, or the Mystery of Providence* (1678)—that were to nurture Protestant preaching and piety well into the future. Sherlock's *Discourse* went through at least twelve editions in Great Britain by the end of the eighteenth century and had also appeared on the European continent in French and German translations. Crossing the Atlantic, it was published several times in North America, mainly under Methodist auspices, between 1823 and 1890. An edition published in Pittsburgh in 1848 carried "recommendatory notices" from leading Methodist, Presbyterian, and Episcopal clergy in that city. Summers's preface to the next edition (published in Richmond in 1854 and again in Nashville in 1856) states that this, the most "practical and permanent" of Sherlock's works, "still holds its value as a text-book on this subject.... We hope that this volume, now put among our standard works, may obtain a wide circulation, and find a place in all our family libraries, as well

---

2. Quoted in O. P. Fitzgerald, *Dr. Summers: A Life-Study* (Nashville: Southern Methodist Publishing House, 1884), 270.

as those of our Sunday-schools and other institutions."[3] A brief unsigned review in the *Methodist Quarterly Review* in April 1854 states, "This is an old book, but of imperishable value. Nothing has yet superseded or equalled it in the particular field which it occupies. All our people should read it for its clear, Scriptural exposition of a subject so deeply and perpetually connected with human happiness."[4]

A copy of the 1856 edition now in the Bridwell Library at Southern Methodist University carries at the bottom of the last page a pencilled notation made by an unidentified (presumably Southern) reader during the final winter of the American Civil War: "Jan. 25th 1865 I finished 1st reading of this book—Thank the Lord for the doctrine of Providence."

Accounts of divine providence, I have suggested, have normally functioned in the Christian tradition to address the question, How are we to understand theologically what goes on? That is, how are we to understand events in their "God-relatedness"? The question itself is inescapable, given what James A. Sanders has called the "monotheizing dynamic" in the literature that makes up the Jewish and Christian Bibles—the pursuit, in that literature, of a vision of "the Integrity of Reality," and of patterns and practices of human life that are in keeping with that integrity.[5] For communities of faith that take that literature as canonical, everything that happens must somehow cohere, and everything that happens must be placed somehow in relation to the reality, will, and work of God.

The question is not merely speculative. To ask how God is related to what goes on is also to ask how we are to relate ourselves to it, and, through it, to God. Like other genuinely theological questions, this one is thoroughly existential and eminently practical. Its existentiality and practicality emerge most strongly when our sense of the integrity of reality is being put to the test, whether in our personal lives or in some broader context.

3. Thomas O. Summers, preface to *A Discourse Concerning the Divine Providence*, by William Sherlock, D.D., 3rd American ed. (Nashville: E. Stevenson & F. A. Owen, Agents for the Methodist Episcopal Church, South, 1856), 2–3.

4. *Methodist Quarterly Review* 8 no. 2 (April 1854): 307.

5. James A. Sanders, *Canon and Community: A Guide to Canonical Criticism* (Philadelphia: Fortress Press, 1984), 56–60.

The simplest, most elegant procedure for answering the question might appear to be to ascribe everything that happens to the will of God, and then to find ways to reconcile such ascription with what the community otherwise holds to be true of God. This has in fact been the favored procedure throughout Christian history, at least at the level of officially sanctioned teaching and its theological elaboration. It was an especially attractive, indeed virtually compelling, procedure at that level during the long period of Western Christian history when some version of Christianity was the established religion of the state, and when notions of divine sovereignty and human imperial sovereignty were fatefully assimilated to one another.[6] In the doctrinal expositions of this entire period, assumptions about divinity that were derived largely from Greco-Roman philosophy tended to function as "control beliefs," effectively ruling out the idea that anything would or could be other than as God intends it.[7] Everything that happens in time is the unfolding of an eternal design. If there is genuine human freedom (as nearly all Christian writers would affirm), it is a freedom whose exercise is entirely in God's hands. Whether God is said to determine our free choices or, rather, to know what those choices will be and to incorporate them into the divine plan, in either case all things proceed according to the divine will, in every particular.

The core of this outlook is probably Stoic in origin.[8] Students of

---

6. While some form of Christianity is still the established or state-supported religion in some countries, in most relevant respects this period is at an end, though we are still contending with its legacy.

7. John E. Sanders, "God As Personal," in *The Grace of God, the Will of Man*, ed. Clark H. Pinnock (Grand Rapids: Zondervan Publishing House, 1989), 168–73, and (with much fuller biblical exegesis) John E. Sanders, *The God Who Risks: A Theology of Providence* (Downers Grove, IL: InterVarsity Press, 1998), 69. Sanders takes the idea of "control beliefs" from Nicholas Wolterstorff, *Reason Within the Bounds of Religion* (Grand Rapids: Wm. B. Eerdmans Publishing Co., 1976).

8. In Gérard Verbeke's apt summary, Stoicism as a widespread religious philosophy offered a doctrine of "internal liberation," accessible equally to everyone regardless of gender, social status, or other outward circumstances. The course of events is fixed, governed by divine reason. Our freedom is realized not in contending with our circumstances but rather in transcending them (with their apparent evils), achieving an indifference to them. Gérard Verbeke, *The Presence of Stoicism in Medieval Thought* (Washington, DC: Catholic University of America Press, 1983), 2–3. In Christian adaptations of Stoicism, the goal was usually more positively stated in terms of harmony with the divine will or union with God. The definitive study of the traces of Stoicism in early Western Christianity is Marcia L. Colish, *The Stoic Tradition from Antiquity to the Early Middle Ages*, vol. 2, *Stoicism in Christian Latin Thought Through the Sixth Century* (Leiden: E. J. Brill, 1985).

the New Testament know that Stoicism was present in Christian thought from its beginnings; it was part of the Hellenistic culture in which Jesus himself lived, and there are apparent allusions to Stoic maxims and ideas in the letters of Paul. Its influence became stronger as Christianity moved into the upper levels of Roman society, and writers schooled in classical thought became the chief interpreters of and apologists for the Christian faith. Stoic themes and concepts were so much a part of the mental furniture of the ancient world that their assimilation into Christian thought and writing was largely unconscious. The Stoic concept of providence appears—indeed, is taken for granted in its main lines—in such early writers as Origen. The concept was shortly to take on new importance with the imperial sanction of the church under Constantine: it provided a point of contact with pagan high culture as well as with more popular ideas, and it enabled Christian apologists to develop accounts of reality that served the now-harmonized interests of church and empire.[9] It continued to serve that function well into the modern period.[10]

Other philosophical traditions, both Platonic and Aristotelian, are

9. See Averil Cameron, "Divine Providence in Late Antiquity," *Predicting the Future*, ed. Leo Howe and Alan Wain (Cambridge: Cambridge University Press, 1993), 118–43. These efforts faced strong resistance. Cameron writes that "the idea of Christian providence constituted a totalising explanation, a kind of theory of everything" (121), and ordinary people tended, then as now, to suspect such neat schemes and to be rather more eclectic in their approaches to life's problems. Although providence was strongly promoted by the authorities of church and empire together, there is abundant evidence of massive "defection" from the idea, for example, in the continuing popularity of the notion of fortune.

10. For example, Barbara Shapiro notes the following regarding John Wilkins's writings: "In 1649 Wilkins published *A Discourse Concerning the Beauty of Providence*, one of his most popular sermons, and the one that, of all his writings, sheds most light on his reaction to the events of the 1640's. The sermon was intended to comfort those who had been adversely affected by the events of the past few years. It was essentially a plea to accept the recent upheavals in Church and State because they had been ordered by God. Although Wilkins says nothing of King and Parliament, or Anglican, Presbyterian, and Independent, it is not difficult to see that he was displeased with the direction events had taken, and that the discourse was written to help others accept a world gone awry. The doctrine of Providence made men cheerful and thankful in times of mercy; in times of suffering it should make them patient and submissive. The doctrine of Providence, as propagated by Wilkins, had many affinities with Stoicism, and was a favorite of those influenced by Roman thought. Wilkins particularly admired the Stoics and was constantly citing 'the divine' Seneca. Of all Wilkins's early writings on religious matters, the sermon on Providence most resembles the later works in its emphasis on the role of reason and natural theology, and its reliance on classical rather than Biblical tradition." Barbara Shapiro, *John Wilkins, 1614–1672: An Intellectual Biography* (Berkeley: University of California Press, 1969), 69–70.

more prominent than Stoicism in Boethius's *The Consolation of Philosophy*, but these are to some degree "Stoicized" (as one commentator puts it[11]). In this, perhaps the most influential treatise on providence in the Western Christian tradition, distinctively Christian elements are either entirely lacking or are so subtle as to evade most readers—a fact that has created a certain amount of debate over the centuries as to whether the author was indeed a Christian (and, if so, what kind of Christian) at the time of its writing.[12] In writings on providence in this tradition, however, the control exercised by the classical philosophical conceptuality is typical, however abundant the scriptural references may be and to whatever particular confessional heritage the writers may belong. We would, perhaps, not be surprised to find the Calvinist Thomas Crane writing, "If contingents were without the bridle of Providence, God should be some petty lord, not an absolute and universal governor over the world."[13] But it is no less obvious to Crane's contemporary, the "Arminian" Anglican William Sherlock, that "the absolute government of all things must be in [God's] hands, or else something might be done which he would not have done."[14] From the *De Ordine* of Augustine and *The Consolation of Philosophy* of Boethius to these classic seventeenth-century Protestant expositions of the doctrine of providence and their later imitations, the tenor of these treatments is unrelentingly optimistic. Everything comes to pass as God wills it, and thus everything is just as it is meant to be. Summers, following Sherlock's logic, could join his fellow "gentlemen theologians" in the antebellum American

---

11. Colish, *The Stoic Tradition*, 267. "The *Consolation* reflects Boethius' belief that classical philosophy contains an authentic wisdom fully compatible with patristic theology and his own Christian faith. The elements involved are combined so thoroughly in Boethius' mind that the specification of their similarities and differences is no longer important for him" (280).

12. On this debate and on the content of the *Consolation* generally, see the studies collected in *Boethius*, ed. Manfred Fuhrmann and Joachim Gruber (Darmstadt: Wissenschaftliche Buchgesellschaft, 1984), especially Ernst Hoffmann, "Griechische Philosophie und christliches Dogma bei Boethius" (278–85).

13. T. C. [Thomas Crane], *Isagoge ad Dei Providentiam, or, A Prospect of Divine Providence* (London: Edward Brewster, 1672), 47 (orthography modernized). John Wesley knew and cited this work and abridged it for his *Christian Library*. There is, incidentally, no record of Wesley's having read Sherlock's discourse on providence; Sherlock may have been too Latitudinarian for his taste.

14. Sherlock, *Discourse*, 36.

South in seeing slavery as providentially ordained;[15] but so, it must be said, could Sherlock's readers in the North and a number of the slaves themselves,[16] though their respective interpretations of the divine intention and its implications for human conduct would differ considerably.

Why did God arrange for the enslavement in America of millions of persons of African descent? Why does God want so many children to die of abuse and neglect? What did God intend by the destruction of the World Trade Center in New York? Moving to a more particular level: Why was it God's will that one person should be killed outright in that latter disaster, that another should receive just the injuries she received, and that a third should have been absent from work on the morning of the attack and thus spared? These questions, once posed, obviously admit of a great many possible answers. The presumption in each case—the presumption on which the entire standard Christian doctrine of providence depends—is that nothing happens that God does not intend. "Permit" or "allow" is not enough, if these words imply that God would have things otherwise.[17] If God would have them otherwise, they would simply *be* otherwise. The alternative—a world in which things are not in God's absolute control—is,

---

15. Summers is briefly discussed in E. Brooks Holifield, *The Gentlemen Theologians: American Theology in Southern Culture 1795–1860* (Durham, NC: Duke University Press, 1978). His sometime pastoral colleague in Charleston, the Presbyterian Thomas Smyth, called slavery "part of the original curse pronounced upon the earth, on man, on woman, and is therefore to be classed among the evils incident to a sinful nature in a sin-polluted world, and a providential remedial agency for accomplishing wise and beneficial results . . ." (quoted in Holifield, 153). Smyth might have been paraphrasing Sherlock when he argued against reformers that we cannot "turn back the course of eternal providence. . . . This order of divine providence affects also our position, circumstances, and sphere of duty, as much as the duty itself. . . . Duty therefore requires us to accept God's arrangements, to acquiesce in them, to act in harmony with them, and not to fall behind or to go beyond them, until in the use of proper means, God opens or shuts the door" (Holifield, 152).

16. See Riggins R. Earl Jr., "Race, Suffering, Slavery, Divine Providence: Some Black and White Deists' and Theists' Voices," in *Christian Faith Seeking Historical Understanding: Essays in Honor of H. Jackson Forstman*, ed. James O. Duke and Anthony L. Dunnavant (Macon, GA: Mercer University Press, 1997), 109–38; Josiah Ulysses Young III, *A Pan-African Theology: Providence and the Legacies of the Ancestors* (Trenton, NJ: Africa World Press, 1992).

17. For Sherlock and many others, such words may rightly be used to distinguish the evil done by a creature from the good God intends to realize through that creaturely action: God "willingly permits" the sin and puts it to good use. Others renounce the concept of permission altogether as misleading.

from the standpoint of the logic of sovereignty at work here, simply absurd.

The seventeenth century was a boom period for the doctrine of providence. The Protestant Reformation and the ensuing theological, political, and social unrest created an urgent and persistent demand for it in several ways, and the resulting literature has been determinative for the doctrine ever since.[18] Sherlock's discourse on providence, along with a few of the other leading expositions from the same era, have been commended, reprinted, excerpted, summarized, and paraphrased for over three hundred years, and we might even now echo the judgment of that mid-nineteenth-century Methodist reviewer: these works have not yet been superseded. Of the several factors that combine to account for this circumstance, two stand out.

First, these were well-designed and effective instruments of popular doctrinal instruction, and they were recognized and employed as such. Their authors were attentive to what is involved in the conveying of doctrine not only as a coherent body of ideas but as a set of life-shaping concepts. They teach the facts of providence, as their authors see them, clearly and persuasively; but they also take care to teach the emotions that go with those facts. Thus they help the reader to understand what it would mean to live by this doctrine—to "get the concept" as a working capacity.[19] Though their particular rhetorics and strategies differ, these treatises are all written to be understood and absorbed by the common reader and to shape that reader's dispositions. Sherlock's work in particular exemplifies the

---

18. See Alexandra Walsham, *Providence in Early Modern England* (Oxford: Oxford University Press, 1999), chap. 1; Kaspar von Greyerz, *Vorsehungsglaube und Kosmologie: Studien zu englischen Selbstzeugnissen des 17. Jahrhunderts* (Göttingen: Vandenhoek & Ruprecht, 1990). Though both are mainly concerned with developments in England, both point to parallels elsewhere.

19. Crane's work approaches this task most systematically. The bulk of it is divided into "observations," each with two chapters. The first enunciates a principle or maxim and illustrates it from Scripture and occasionally from later history; the second indicates what the principle implies for the life of the Christian, often in the form of admonitions: be content, be consoled, be watchful. Flavel's work is filled with concrete illustration and exhortation to the same end. Even Sherlock's, which Thomas Jackson (see note 21 below) called "more argumentative and less practical" than these others, is clearly intended to shape the attitudes and dispositions of its readers, and to give them what Sherlock would call a "sense" of providence, as distinct from a "mere belief." (On this distinction, see William Sherlock, *A Practical Discourse Concerning a Future Judgment* [London: W. Rogers, 1692], 189.)

"plain style" of late-seventeenth-century English prose, a style for whose rise John Wilkins himself was notably responsible, and one that mediated theological as well as scientific knowledge to the general culture. In some ways, the style and the content of Sherlock's discourses were admirably suited to each other and to the emerging modern sensibility.[20]

The second notable factor in the longevity of these works is simply that, in large part because of their formative standing, they have had no serious rivals in the past three centuries. Well into the twentieth century, they were reprinted by denominational presses, endorsed by pastors, reviewed and recommended in church periodicals, and disseminated through the churches' publishing agencies. Imitated at times, they were never replaced.[21] Even now, they exercise a powerful residual influence.

This may seem a strange thing to say. The doctrine of providence has been in serious trouble since these treatises were first published. Our expanding knowledge of the universe has rendered its anthropocentrism extremely implausible. Modern biblical scholarship has rendered its appeals to Scripture for support untenable. And its content and implications are widely felt to be morally repugnant. The standard doctrine of providence inculcated by these classics has long since ceased to operate as a central guiding principle in the lives of

---

20. On the "plain style" and on these writers' employment of it, see W. Fraser Mitchell, *English Pulpit Oratory from Andrewes to Tillotson* (London: S.P.C.K., 1932) and especially Robert Adolph, *The Rise of Modern Prose Style* (Cambridge, MA: M.I.T. Press, 1968). Irène Simon's *Three Restoration Divines: Barrow, South, Tillotson*, vol. 1 (Paris: Société d'Edition "Les Belles Lettres," 1967) is helpful on the shift in modes of argument (see esp. chap. 2, "Anglican Rationalism in the Seventeenth Century," 75–148), as is Gerard Reedy's *The Bible and Reason: Anglicans and Scripture in Late Seventeenth-Century England* (Philadelphia: University of Pennsylvania Press, 1985). Barbara Shapiro (*Probability and Certainty in Seventeenth-Century England* [Princeton: Princeton University Press, 1983]) perceptively relates religious, scientific, and literary developments (see especially 252 ff.); see also her *John Wilkins, 1614–1672: An Intellectual Biography*. Ian Green, in *Print and Protestantism in Early Modern England* (Oxford: Oxford University Press, 2000), studies the publishing history and readership of a sample of "best-sellers" and "steady sellers," including several of Sherlock's books.

21. Among nineteenth-century "updates" might be mentioned Thomas Jackson's *The Providence of God Viewed in the Light of Holy Scripture*, 2nd ed. (London: Wesleyan Conference Office, 1866), and Jonathan Weaver's *Divine Providence* (Dayton, Ohio: United Brethren Publishing House, 1872). Of the originals, only Flavel's work is currently in print, thanks to a Banner of Truth Trust edition that has been steadily reprinted since 1963.

many Christians living in the modern West. The questions stated a few paragraphs earlier (on the model of "Why has God brought this about?") would strike these Christians believers not as pious and pertinent, but rather as blasphemous and misleading.

Despite all this, it is fair to say that the standard doctrine of providence is still a powerful force. In many conservative and evangelical Christian traditions throughout the world—often in conscious resistance to modernity in all its aspects—the doctrine is sincerely held and vigorously taught and professed.[22] However, in those more liberal traditions in which it is no longer affirmed and cultivated, it has not simply disappeared. Three centuries of discontent with the standard doctrine of providence has often expressed itself not in active critique and reconstruction but rather in passive avoidance and, as a frequent companion, cognitive and emotional dissonance. The doctrine remains in place; it is deeply ingrained in the churches' traditions, piety, and practice and has not been supplanted there. It is represented in the normative doctrinal heritage of a good many Christian denominations, including those in the Wesleyan tradition.[23] It is written into their hymnody and liturgy. It comes almost automatically to the surface in times of crisis, as members of a congregation struggle to provide consolation and support to one another. For better or

---

22. This is not true of all conservative or evangelical Christians, of course. A lively revisionist approach is currently being argued by such theologians as Clark Pinnock and John Sanders—apparently a serious-enough movement to have earned the formal censure of the Evangelical Theological Society at a recent annual meeting.

23. I mention the Wesleyan tradition in particular because, as a life-long Methodist, I am aware that many Methodists regard the doctrine of providence in general as something alien—Calvinist, perhaps. But the doctrine of these seventeenth-century writers is one that, in its main lines, John Wesley assumed and taught. Although Wesley himself makes no reference to Sherlock's discourse (he was suspicious of Sherlock on other grounds), Sherlock's way of reconciling human freedom with the divine ordering of all events would have been compatible with Wesley's own commitments. See, e.g., Wesley's treatment of "persecution" as God's work in his third discourse on the Sermon on the Mount (*The Works of John Wesley*, vol. 1, *Sermons I*, ed. Albert C. Outler [Nashville: Abingdon Press, 1984]), especially 523–25. A sample: "There is no one branch of God's government of the world which is more to be admired than this. His ear is never heavy to the threatenings of the persecutor, or the cry of the persecuted. His eye is ever open, and his hand stretched out to direct even the minutest circumstance. When the storm shall begin, how high it shall rise, which way it shall point its course, when and how it shall end, are all determined by his unerring wisdom. The ungodly are only a sword of his; an instrument which he uses as it pleaseth him, and which itself, when the gracious ends of his providence are answered, is cast into the fire."

worse, then, what we have in these classic texts has a fair claim to be regarded still as the established and recognized teaching of the churches regarding the providence of God—whether deliberately or by default.

For all of its learned consistency and ecclesial support, this official line of teaching has always been received with something short of universal approbation. To be sure, many have found it profoundly consoling. Others have done their best to accept it, believing that any difficulties they may have with it are difficulties in *them* (the believers) and not difficulties in *it* (the doctrine). But others have found it impossible to accept. Some—as their circumstances permit—have left the church on this account. Others have followed the time-honored practice of "defecting in place"—a new name, perhaps, for a very old phenomenon.[24] It is common, but it may also be quite mistaken, to regard the resistance of ordinary Christians to certain official Christian doctrines as evidence of residual paganism or incomplete Christianization. In some cases, at least, their resistance may mean just the opposite. Rather than buy into a churchly sanctioned doctrine that appears to them to do violence to the gospel and to themselves, they may seek out or develop on their own the resources to sustain a more acceptable alternative.

A Reorientation

The great liberal church historian Adolf von Harnack, like most great historians not lacking in a sense of irony, remarks somewhere that while at first Christianity was Trinitarian in its piety but monotheistic in its doctrine of God, within a few centuries it became Trinitarian in its doctrine but monotheistic in its piety.[25] On Harnack's reading of developments, the first Christians lived out of a vivid experience

---

24. For a range of contemporary examples, see *Defecting In Place: Women Claiming Responsibility for Their Own Spiritual Lives*, ed. Miriam Therese Winter, Adair Lummis, and Allison Stokes (New York: Crossroad Publishing Company, 1994).

25. I have been unable to locate this remark in Harnack's work, but an argument for the substance of it could certainly be reconstructed from his 1899–1900 lectures *What Is Christianity?* translated by Thomas Bailey Saunders (2nd ed.; New York: G. P. Putnam's Sons, 1901).

of God through Jesus Christ and in the Holy Spirit, but they did so in a Jewish environment that insisted that God is one. As Christianity moved into a less Jewish and more Greek religious and cultural ethos, it intellectualized its experience of God, yielding to the pressures of the new ethos and using Greek philosophical resources to work out a fully articulated doctrine of the Trinity. Meanwhile, the strong monotheistic piety of that same Greek culture—perhaps sensing a vacuum at the experiential level—succeeded in supplanting the original, more complex Trinitarian piety of the earlier Christians.[26]

Much in Harnack's account of the first few centuries of Christian history has been called seriously into question, including the various dichotomies built into it (dichotomies, for example, between Greek and Hebrew mentalities, and between piety and doctrine or experience and thought). But there is some justice to his observation, at least so far as the doctrine of providence is concerned. It is as if there were two parallel processes at work in those early centuries. On the one hand, Christian thinkers were working to explicate and clarify the Trinitarian "grammar" of Christian discourse—a grammar that had already been implicitly informing that discourse from New Testament times onward. The Trinitarian rules for talking about God and about God's activity that were endorsed by major ecumenical councils are the result of that process. On the other hand, Christian thinkers—sometimes the same ones—were developing (or adapting from pagan sources) accounts of God's providence that seemed to have little to do with these same Trinitarian commitments.

This dissociation of providence from Trinitarian considerations may help to explain the subsequent career of providence as a doctrinal locus. In systematic theology, on the whole, providence has been "appropriated" to the Father,[27] and its treatment is largely uninformed by christological or pneumatological considerations. It is typically

26. "So much depth and delicacy of feeling, so much earnestness and dignity, and—above all—so strong a *monotheistic* piety were displayed in the religious ethics of the Greeks, acquired as it had been by hard toil on a basis of inner experience and metaphysical speculation, that the Christian religion could not pass by this treasure with indifference" (Harnack, *What Is Christianity?*, 216–17).

27. John Wesley follows this convention of locating providence in the "first article" in his sermon, "Catholic Spirit," in *The Works of John Wesley*, vol. 2, *Sermons II*, ed. Albert C. Outler (Nashville: Abingdon Press, 1985), 87.

lodged within or appended to the doctrine of creation, where its chief function is to state that the same God who created the world sustains and cares for it. This creator-sustainer God often looks a great deal like the Supreme Being of philosophical theism, and indeed in many theological traditions providence, like creation, is regarded as a doctrine whose content can be known by natural reason, or "by the light of nature." Such structural features serve to reinforce the isolation of the doctrine from specifically Christian commitments and its liability to external control.

"Long ago God spoke to our ancestors in many and various ways by the prophets," observes the author of Hebrews, "but in these last days he has spoken to us by a Son, whom he appointed heir of all things, through whom he also created the worlds" (Heb. 1:1–2). There is certainly ample variety in the ways the biblical writings speak to the question of providence. Ranging from the claim that nothing happens that God does not make happen (e.g., Isa. 45:7) to the claim that there is a good deal of sheer contingency to events (e.g., Eccl. 9:11–12), these various ways resist and subvert harmonization.[28] In introducing his early study of a closely related theme, that of suffering, James Sanders noted, "There are some eight solutions found in the Old Testament to the problem of suffering. Briefly, sufferings are retributive, disciplinary, revelational, probational, illusory (or transitory), mysterious (only God has Wisdom), eschatological, or meaningless."[29] The phenomenon of canonization functions to preserve rather than eliminate this variety. The "monotheizing dynamic" of which Sanders was later to speak operates not despite but precisely in and through this conflict of understandings. The book of Job is the exemplification and, in a way, a culmination of this biblical strategy.

---

28. For a brief analysis of the variety, see Frank-Lothar Hossfeld, "Wie sprechen die Heiligen Schriften, insbesondere das Alte Testament, von der Vorsehung Gottes?"in *Vorsehung und Handeln Gottes*, ed. Theodor Schneider and Lothar Ullrich (Freiburg: Herder, 1988), 72–93. Hossfeld concludes that it is impossible to construct a coherent general theory of providence from the Bible—and that perhaps this impossibility is a clue as to how these materials might properly function for us. He takes the language of Heb. 1:1—"*viele* Male und auf *vielerlei Weise* hat Gott einst zu den Vätern gesprochen durch die Propheten" (72, italics his)—to suggest that we do well to speak of "the holy scriptures" in the plural and to respect rather than downplay their differences.

29. Jim Alvin Sanders, *Suffering As Divine Discipline in the Old Testament and Post-Biblical Judaism*, a special issue of the Colgate Rochester Divinity School Bulletin 28 (1955): 1.

God's speaking to us "by a Son" was anticipated by Job's "speaking rightly" of God (Job 42:7–9), as a number of commentators have observed;[30] and in both cases the "speaking" transcends words. Doing anything like justice to what is revealed about the God-relatedness of events in these two figures, and in the canonical witness taken as a whole, is no light task. The understanding of God (if one may properly speak of "understanding" in this connection[31]) that emerges from a genuine encounter with these materials must reflect a certain complexity, as both Jewish and Christian traditions testify.

Blaise Pascal was not mistaken in his *mémoriale*: The monotheism proper to these traditions is a far cry from the abstract, generic theism of modern philosophical discussion. A number of contemporary theologians have labeled this latter theism, when it appears in Christian guise, a heresy.[32] But it is not difficult to understand why many people within as well as outside these traditions might tend to confuse the two. The God of modern theism is the heir of the "God of providence" of the long Constantinian period. It is a concept of God profoundly alienated from Christian Trinitarian experience and understanding, despite their long coexistence.[33]

Far from being an abandonment of monotheistic faith, the doctrine of the Trinity represents its Christian form. As James Sanders puts it, the development of Trinitarian doctrine was the early Christian attempt to monotheize.[34] That doctrine honors the integrity of reality by recognizing its inherent complexity. It aims to provide a suffi-

---

30. Notable among the more recent are Karl Barth (*Church Dogmatics* IV/3, part 1 [Edinburgh: T. & T. Clark, 1961], 384) and Gustavo Gutiérrez (*On Job: God-Talk and the Suffering of the Innocent*, trans. Matthew J. O'Connell [Maryknoll, NY: Orbis Books, 1987]).

31. "Si comprehendis, non est Deus," said Augustine. In a number of ways, Jewish and Christian rules and conventions for referring to God are meant to reinforce this very point. We operate in this area with a variety of concepts and "understandings" that we take (in hope) to provide sufficient guidance for the purpose at hand, but they do not finally add up to a "grasp" of the divine reality. See Paul DeHart, "The Ambiguous Infinite: Jüngel, Marion, and the God of Descartes," *Journal of Religion* 82 (2002): 75–96); R. Kendall Soulen, "The Name of the Holy Trinity: A Triune Name," *Theology Today* 59 (2002): 244–61; Humphrey Palmer, *Analogy: A Study of Qualification and Argument in Theology* (New York: St. Martin's Press, 1973).

32. Nicholas Lash, "Considering the Trinity," *Modern Theology* 2 (1986): 183–96.

33. Michael J. Buckley, S.J.'s, *At the Origins of Modern Atheism* (New Haven, CT: Yale University Press, 1987) illuminates these connections and disconnections brilliantly.

34. James A. Sanders, *Canon and Community: A Guide to Canonical Criticism* (Philadelphia: Fortress Press, 1984), 59.

ciently rich set of rules for referring to God and for referring all things to God. But "monotheizing" is an ongoing and never-ending struggle. The standard doctrine of providence represents a massive and chronic failure on the part of the church to monotheize its understanding of God's relation to events in accord with its own Trinitarian insights.

What might a doctrine of providence honoring Trinitarian commitments look like?

The Second Council of Constantinople (conventionally reckoned as the fifth ecumenical council, meeting in 553), in its opening statement on the triunity of God, affirmed the "one nature or substance" of the Father, Son, and Holy Spirit, "their one virtue and power, a consubstantial Trinity," and added, "For there is one God and Father, from whom are all things, and one Lord Jesus Christ, through whom are all things, and one Holy Spirit, in whom are all things."[35] With this latter statement the council was not innovating but endorsing a rule of Trinitarian grammar regarding the "economy" of God, that is, God's action *ad extra*, that had been worked out some time before.[36] In doing so, it was invoking an insight lodged in the "depth grammar" of Christian doctrine: God relates to things "triunely."

This insight yields several implications for the construction of a Christian doctrine of providence. Most, if not all, of these have been acknowledged and explored at some point in the history of the doctrine but have then been subordinated to the logic of sovereignty controlling the standard doctrine, so their potential for transformation has been left unrealized. One such implication is that God's relation to what goes on is coherent but complex, and that the complexity demands and deserves attention. The most visible and promising

---

35. Canons of the Second Council of Constantinople (553), in *Documents of the Christian Church*, 3rd ed., ed. Henry Bettenson and Chris Maunder (New York: Oxford University Press, 1999), 100. Cf. Denzinger, *Enchiridion Symbolorum*, par. 213.

36. For a key statement, see Gregory of Nyssa, "On Not Three Gods" (composed ca. 390): "Ad Ablabium, Quod Non Sint Tres Dei," in *Gregorii Nysseni Opera Dogmatica Minora*, part 1, ed. Frederick Mueller (Leiden: E. J. Brill, 1958), 47–48. Some recent translations of this admittedly difficult work seem to obscure the force of the three crucial prepositions, *ek* (from), *di'* (through), and *en* (in). The old Nicene and Post-Nicene Fathers (NPNF) version, while perhaps problematic in some other ways, does not.

trace of this implication in the history of the doctrine is the emergence and widespread (though not universal) acceptance of the familiar threefold distinction within the concept of providence: the work of providence is at one and the same time *conservatio*, *gubernatio*, and *concursus*, or "upholding," "governing," and "cooperating." Thinking through this complexity with some close attention to the doctrine of the Trinity, and particularly to the "prepositional logic" of the conciliar statement cited above (from the Father, through the Son, in the Spirit), might be a revolutionary step, particularly if it is taken in conjunction with a second implication. This one, so far as I am aware, hardly figures in standard treatments of the doctrine. It is simply that the triune pattern of God's relation to all things is also the pattern of our knowledge of that relation. To the extent that we can understand how God is related to what goes on, we understand it "through Jesus Christ" and "in the Holy Spirit."

We will turn in succeeding chapters to a fuller exploration of these suggestions. The range of possibilities they open up can be hinted at, however, by a brief quotation from the Anglican theologian Dorothy L. Sayers, who (in her other vocation as mystery writer) furnished the epigraph for this chapter. Writing on the implications of the doctrine of the incarnation for our attitudes toward "matter," Sayers writes,

> The Church . . . must insist strongly that the whole material universe is an expression and incarnation of the creative energy of God, as a book or a picture is the material expression of the creative soul of the artist. For that reason, all good and creative handling of the material universe is holy and beautiful, and all abuse of the material universe is a crucifixion of the body of Christ.[37]

Another vital implication of the confession that "all things" are from, through, and in God must be mentioned: there is a radical unity to the work or action of God *ad extra*. Writers such as Sherlock and Crane were well aware of the conventional division of the external activity of God into two works, creation and providence, and also of the concession by many writers that this division is an artifice for the sake of exposition and that the two are essentially one. "There is an

---

37. Dorothy L. Sayers, *Creed or Chaos?* (New York: Harcourt, Brace & Co., 1949), 42.

indissoluble or firm knot knit betwixt the Lord's creating and governing the world," observes Crane, "for what is providence but a kind of continued creation?"[38] But no sooner is the point made than it is left behind. Sherlock writes, "It is a vain inquiry of the schools, which no man can resolve, and which serves no end in religion, whether creation and preservation be the same or two different acts." He goes on to make the distinction that is determinative in nearly all standard expositions: "This much is certain: to create is to give being to that which was not before; to preserve, is to continue that in being which was made before; and when any thing is once created, it cannot be newly created, for to create is to make out of nothing, not to make a thing which already is."[39] Sherlock's Lutheran and Reformed contemporaries on the continent were issuing the same sort of disclaimer: God does not continue to create. Creation is complete, as the Genesis account of the first week makes clear (they pointed especially to Gen. 2:1–3, with its repeated emphasis on "finished"). If providence is to be called a continuation of creation, we must be careful (the disclaimer says) to specify this as God's continuation or holding in being of what has already been created, and not as a continuation of the activity of creation.[40] Some writers, apparently sensing a danger even in the highly qualified use of the idea, eventually went beyond the disclaimer to deny that it is appropriate to call providence "creation continued" in any sense, lest the important distinction between the finished work of creation and the ongoing work of providence be compromised.[41]

In effect, providence has been severed from creation. Providence has been allocated the time "in between" the world's creation and its

38. Crane, *Isagoge ad Dei Providentiam*, 5.

39. Sherlock, *A Discourse Concerning the Divine Providence*, 24–25.

40. See Heinrich Schmid, *The Doctrinal Theology of the Evangelical Lutheran Church*, 3rd ed., trans. Charles A. Hay and Henry E. Jacobs (Minneapolis: Augsburg Publishing House, 1961), 179; Heinrich Heppe, *Reformed Dogmatics*, rev. and ed. Ernst Bizer, trans. G. T. Thompson (Grand Rapids: Baker Book House, 1978), 257. J. A. Quenstedt, following J. F. König, seems willing to take the relation more seriously: "God preserves all things by the continuation of the action by which He first produced them. For the preservation of a thing is, properly speaking, nothing else than a continued production of it, *nor do they differ except by a designation derived from without*" (quoted in Schmid, *Doctrinal Theology,* 179).

41. Chr. Ernst Luthardt, *Kompendium der Dogmatik*, 10th ed. (Leipzig: Dörffling & Franke, 1900), sect. 34, "Das Verhältnis Gottes zur geschaffenen Welt (De providentia)," 142.

consummation—between creation and new creation, we might say—and has been drained of any creative significance. It is no accident, then, that the emphasis in the doctrine is on preservation, stability, order, and harmony, and that the virtues it inculcates are mainly passive. Our duty under God's providence is to adjust to the way things are, to accept the order of things, and to receive with all humility and gratitude what God sends us. To say, as Sherlock does, that the question of the relation of creation and providence "serves no end in religion" is a tragic mistake.

To recapture the unity of creation and providence—the creative character of providence and the providential character of creation—might aid in the liberation of the doctrine of providence from its long captivity to "the way things are."[42] It might give the doctrine a better chance than it has ordinarily had to serve the ends of God rather than those of earthly sovereigns of one sort or another. If there is any proper sense in which creation is "finished" (and this depends in large part on what one makes of *creatio ex nihilo*), there is a very important sense in which it is not finished; its finishing, like its beginning, is ongoing. The enigmatic words of the Johannine Jesus, as he explained his willingness to heal on the Sabbath, are worth pondering in this connection: "'My Father is still working, and I also am working'" (John 5:17).

Finally, to view creation and providence, and, for that matter, new creation, *together* as one ongoing work, one eternal act of God being realized throughout time and space, might not only renew the doctrine of providence but also provide new perspective on every other aspect of the Christian witness.

---

42. A probing recent study of this captivity is Roque Frangiotti, *A doutrina tradicional da providencia: implicacões sociopoliticas* (São Paulo: Ediciones Paulinas, 1986).

Chapter 4

The Grammar of Providence

*L*et us assume that the question the Christian doctrine of providence addresses is this: "How are we to understand theologically what goes on?" The very name of the doctrine suggests the main direction the answer to this question is to take, or at any rate the direction it has generally taken: "Consider that, in everything that goes on, God is providing." (Note the difference between the claim "God is providing everything that goes on" and the claim "God is providing *in* everything that goes on." This crucial difference is sometimes overlooked.)

"Providing" is (at least in this context) an action word. God is understood to be doing something. In classical dogmatics, providence is often identified alongside creation as one of the two main "works" or "actions" of God *ad extra*, that is, works involving something other than God. If the doctrine of creation has to do with understanding God as the author or source of the world, the doctrine of providence has to do with understanding God as working in and with the world— or so it has commonly been thought. This doctrinal locus, then, houses the consideration of *how* God may be said to act in and with the world, insofar as Christian faith and reflection have to deal with that issue. Moreover, it centers that consideration on the concept of God's providing. This chapter aims to explore the question of how God's providential activity is best conceived. Dealing with this question will help to expose something of the "depth grammar" of the Christian doctrine of providence.

The concepts of action and activity are notoriously broad and abstract. The philosopher Morris Weitz, following some implications in the work of J. L. Austin, makes a convincing case that the concept of human action is an "open concept" in the sense that although we may identify sufficient conditions for its application, no necessary conditions for it may be specified. That is, no inherent features of "human action" are to be found in every single instance of what may rightly be called by that term.[1] Given the dependence of our talk of divine action on our talk of human action, the same is likely to be true of the concept of divine action. By focusing on the concept of God's providing (broad and complex as that concept may turn out to be) and on some basic features of that providing, we may attain some helpful specification in the discussion of God's activity in the world. But even at that, we should not expect things to be too neat.

Two interesting ways the concept of human (and, by implication, divine) action is open are worth noting at the outset. The first is its openness in the direction of things agents "do" without acting, or even precisely by not acting, in a more strict sense of "acting": some instances of "neglecting," "failing," "allowing," and the like might be mentioned here, along with some instances of "waiting" and the like, "hearing" and the like, and others. One may be held responsible for (or credited with) allowing something to happen, the usual implication being that it was within one's power not to allow it, so that the allowing was something one did. If I am asked, "What did you do when she didn't show up?" it is perfectly appropriate for me to say, "I waited." And "hearing" is often taken to be something one does, even though it does not usually have the active connotations that "listening" carries.

The second direction of the openness of the concept is toward a broad range of what might almost be called "non-agential," or at any rate non-personal-agential, activities: "The meal restored his strength." "The minerals here give the water its distinctive taste." Here the "doing" amounts to having an effect. Some of the activity of personal agents is like the activity of chemical "agents" or other impersonal entities or forces: the influence of presence, the weight of

---

1. Morris Weitz, *The Opening Mind: A Philosophical Study of Humanistic Concepts* (Chicago: University of Chicago Press, 1977), 141–87.

reputation, and the effects of prior deeds may all bear on other creatures in ways that we commonly describe using language implying that the source of the effect "did it" and is in some sense responsible for it, even though we might not want to ascribe the effect to the agent as an act, exactly, nor hold the agent morally responsible. (Take, for example, this: "I used to hold that view, but N. N. changed my mind; she brought me to see the problems in that position and made me understand things differently." Depending on the circumstances, just what sort of acting or activity should be ascribed to N. N. will vary, as will the kind and degree—if any—of responsibility she might rightly be said to have for my change of mind and my present understanding.)

Ludwig Wittgenstein, whose philosophical work combined close conceptual analysis with a constant awareness of the danger of expecting too much clarity and precision in human concepts, wrote, "A main cause of philosophical disease—a one-sided diet: one nourishes one's thinking with only one kind of example."[2] In considering the activity of God, it is well to heed this warning. In a critique of the overemphasis on certain models of personal agency in philosophical discussion of the "acts of God," James M. Gustafson cites some typical ways of speaking of God in the Psalms, Job, and other Wisdom literature and concludes, "It is at least arguable that in these and other places God is interpreted [as] power and order, related to the world less as actor than as impersonal reality to be confronted and to be praised."[3] The analogies for divine activity may need to be drawn from a wider range of creaturely examples than philosophers and theologians are accustomed to use if we are to be attentive to the scope of biblical testimony and to the reality to which it testifies.

Christian theology, as a churchly responsibility, seeks to test the validity of Christian teaching and practice to make sure that it is, as

---

2. Ludwig Wittgenstein, *Philosophical Investigations*, 3rd ed., trans. G. E. M. Anscombe (New York: Macmillan Co., 1958), par. 593.

3. James M. Gustafson, "Alternative Conceptions of God," in *The God Who Acts: Philosophical and Theological Explorations*, ed. Thomas F. Tracy (University Park, PA: University of Pennsylvania Press, 1994), 64–65. James Barr likewise advocates a more comprehensive view of biblical portrayals of the character of God's relation to the world in "Divine Action and Hebrew Wisdom," in *The Making and Remaking of Christian Doctrine: Essays in Honour of Maurice Wiles*, ed. Sarah Coakley and David A. Pailin (Oxford: Clarendon Press, 1993), 1–12.

nearly as possible, what it should be. Such testing involves three distinct but interrelated lines of inquiry: inquiry into the Christian authenticity, the truth, and the fittingness of that teaching and practice. About a given doctrinal formulation, moral pronouncement, or individual or corporate act that aims to embody or express something of the Christian witness, theology asks, Is the witness thus embodied or expressed genuinely Christian? Is it intelligible and (in whatever sense is pertinent) true? Is it fitting to its context—that is, it is suited to have the effect, in that context, that an embodiment or expression of the gospel should have?[4]

The Christian doctrine of providence, at least in its traditional formulations, has long faced serious challenges on all three counts. On the matter of intelligibility and truth, there is, for example, the question—raised in manifold ways—of whether any sense can be given to the notion of God's activity in the world. On the matter of fittingness, it has, for example, been charged that the doctrine as commonly taught and embedded in the lives of believers tends in many situations to encourage passivity and resignation in those who are relatively powerless and to intensify their sense of guilt and worthlessness, while at the same time fostering a sense of well-being and self-satisfaction among the relatively powerful—not exactly the effects one would naturally associate with the teachings of Jesus as represented by the Gospels. And by no means least, the Christian credentials of what passes for the Christian doctrine of providence have from time to time been directly called into question, notably in the recent past by Karl Barth. Writing of "the older Protestant theology" (that is, the Lutheran and Reformed dogmatics from the late sixteenth to the early eighteenth century), Barth observed "the astonishing fact" of its "almost total failure even to ask concerning the Christian meaning and character of the doctrine of providence, let alone to assert it."[5] For Barth, the doctrine of providence has throughout the history of the church been insufficiently informed by what should be the starting point of all Christian talk about God, namely, God's self-revelation in Jesus

---

4. This understanding of the task of Christian theology is elaborated in Charles M. Wood, *Vision and Discernment: An Orientation in Theological Study* (Atlanta: Scholars Press, 1985).

5. Karl Barth, *Church Dogmatics* III/3, trans. G. W. Bromiley and R. J. Ehrlich (Edinburgh: T. & T. Clark, 1960), 30.

Christ. It tends therefore to operate with an insufficiently Christian understanding of God. Barth elaborates:

> The orthodox Lutheran and Reformed teachers are . . . at one in teaching the divine lordship over all occurrence both as a whole and in detail without attempting to say what is the meaning and purpose of this lordship. They understand it as the act of a superior and absolutely omniscient, omnipotent and omnioperative being whose nature and work do of course display such moral qualities as wisdom, righteousness and goodness, etc. But this is all. According to the agreed doctrine of orthodoxy, this empty shell is the object of the Christian belief in providence.[6]

Barth's own rearticulation of the doctrine of providence was not only christological but also Trinitarian in character. He has been followed in this by a number of contemporary theologians, who believe, as one of them puts it, that "an emphasis on God as Trinity gives providence a different face."[7] Recently, there have been signs of some new interest in a Trinitarian approach to the question of how God's action in the world is to be understood,[8] and it is this question in particular that I wish to pursue here, with a specific focus on a Trinitarian understanding of God's providing.

Of course, the "older Protestant theology" by no means denied that it is none other than the triune God who provides. Rather, following the ancient principle that whatever God does *ad extra* is done by the entire Trinity, it typically asserted that providence, like creation, is the "work of the entire Trinity," the "activity of the triune God." However, it has been justly observed that the principle followed here has usually led to an implicit denial that the doctrine of the Trinity has any bearing on our understanding of God's work in the world. Because the works of God *ad extra* are not to be divided up among the persons

---

6. Ibid., 31.

7. Daniel L. Migliore, *Faith Seeking Understanding: An Introduction to Christian Theology* (Grand Rapids: Wm. B. Eerdmans Publishing Co., 1991), 116.

8. See, for example, Christoph Schwöbel, "Die Rede vom Handeln Gottes im christlichen Glauben," *Marburger Jahrbuch Theologie* 1 (1987): 56–81; idem, "Divine Action and Christian Faith," in *God: Action and Revelation* (Kampen: Kok Pharos Publishing House, 1992), 23–45; Werner Brändle, "Überlegungen zur Rede vom Handeln Gottes," *Neue Zeitschrift für systematische Theologie und Religionsphilosophie* 37 (1995): 96–117; and, in a different mode, Bruno Forte, *Trinità come storia*, 3rd ed. (Milan: Edizioni Paoline, 1985).

of the Trinity, theologians have tended to ignore the Trinity when it comes to understanding God's works, and have, in effect, produced "unitarian" accounts of God's involvement with the world.[9] By a strange irony, then, rather than leading to an understanding of how God acts "triunely," the principle that all of God's works *ad extra* are the work of the entire Trinity seems to have encouraged theologians to think of God's action as if God were *not* triune. In consequence, they have tended to stress the notion of God's acting *on* the world, and this is precisely where many of the problems arise to which all three areas of theological critique point: that is, problems regarding the intelligibility and fittingness as well as the authenticity of the account. To the extent that not only the older Protestant theology but also the newer has fallen into this tendency, the doctrine of providence has borne the consequences; and so have all those whose lives have been affected by it.

Yet embedded within the structure of the received doctrine in its most common form lies the key to its proper Trinitarian reconception as a doctrine of the triune activity of God. God's providing, according to this doctrine, is a matter of God's sustaining creation in its own activity, cooperating with or concurring in that activity, and directing the outcomes of that activity for the well-being of creation and for God's own glory.[10] If this threefold scheme can be understood precisely as the *form* of God's providential activity—as the triune struc-

---

9. For the most influential modern formulation of this critique, see Karl Rahner, "Der Dreifaltiger Gott als tranzendenter Urgrund der Heilsgeschichte," in *Mysterium Salutis: Grundriss heilsgeschichtlicher Dogmatik*, ed. Johannes Feiner and Magnus Löhrer, vol. 2, *Die Heilsgeschichte vor Christus* (Einsiedeln: Benziger Verlag, 1967), esp. 319–27. And for an illuminating analysis and criticism of some important aspects of Rahner's own thinking on this matter, see Phillip Cary, "On Behalf of Classical Trinitarianism: A Critique of Rahner on the Trinity," *The Thomist* 56 (1992): 365–405.

10. Cf. the summary definition by J. A. Quenstedt, perhaps the most influential Lutheran dogmatician of the period of "high orthodoxy": "Providentia est actio externa totius ss. trinitatis, qua res a se conditas universas ac singulis tam quoad speciem, quam quoad individua potentissime conservat inque earum actiones et effectus coinfluit ac libere ac sapienter omnia gubernat ad sui gloriam et universi hujus atque imprimis piorum utilitatem ac salutem" (Johann Andreas Quenstedt, *Theologia Didactico-Polemica*, 4th ed. [Wittenberg, 1701], vol. 1, 535). As translated by Schubert M. Ogden: "Providence is the external action of the entire Trinity whereby 1. God most efficaciously upholds the things created, both as an entirety and singly, both in species and in individuals; 2. concurs in their actions and results; and 3. freely and wisely governs all things to his own glory and the welfare and safety of the universe, and especially of the godly." With Quenstedt, the threefold scheme became standard in Lutheran dog-

ture of God's providing—then we might be able to take some initial steps toward a genuinely Christian doctrine of providence. The possibility I wish to explore, then, is that the common threefold structure of the doctrine of providence bears witness to its underlying Trinitarian grammar and can be explicated in such a way as to make that grammar manifest.

The first point to be made in this connection is simply a corrective to the usual construal of the principle about the indivisibility of God's external works: to say that all of God's activity *ad extra* involves the entire Trinity is *not* to say that each member of the Trinity is not involved in that activity in a distinctive way. That there is a triune character or pattern to the work of God is an ancient insight, long obscured but being retrieved in some contemporary theology and spirituality. It appears for example in Nicholas Lash's reference to a Trinitarian view of creation as "founded, focused, and finished" in God,[11] as it did earlier in the writings—prescient in some respects— of Austin M. Farrer. One of the most illuminating testimonies to it in the early church (excluding New Testament materials) is found in Gregory of Nyssa's short treatise "On Not Three Gods":

> We do not learn that the Father does something on his own, in which the Son does not co-operate. Or again, that the Son acts on his own, without the Spirit. Rather does every operation which extends from God to creation and is designated according to our differing conceptions of it have its origin from the Father, proceed through the Son, and reach its completion in the Holy Spirit. It is for this reason that the word for the operation is not divided among the persons involved. For the action of each in any matter is not

---

matics; both it and the older twofold division (without the element of "concurrence") were to be found in Reformed dogmatics. Quenstedt takes this scheme, as well as much of the substance and wording of the "didactic" part of his dogmatics overall, from the *Theologia Positiva Acroamatica* (1664) of Johann Friedrich König. On König's doctrine of providence and its reception, see Carl Heinz Ratschow, *Lutherische Dogmatik zwischen Reformation und Aufklärung*, part 2 (Gütersloh: Gütersloher Verlagshaus Gerd Mohn, 1966), 208–47. König's textbook is now available in a critical edition, with a facing German translation: Johann Friedrich König, *Theologia Positiva Acroamatica (Rostock 1664)*, ed. and trans. Andreas Stegmann (Tübingen: Mohr Siebeck, 2006). A companion volume offers an illuminating account of König's work in the context of early modern Protestant theological reflection and doctrinal instruction: Andreas Stegmann, *Johann Friedrich König* (Tübingen: Mohr Siebeck, 2006).

11. Nicholas Lash, *Believing Three Ways in One God: A Reading of the Apostles' Creed* (Notre Dame, IN: University of Notre Dame Press, 1992), 51–55.

separate and individualized. But whatever occurs, whether in reference to God's providence for us or to the government and constitution of the universe, occurs through the three Persons, and is not three separate things.[12]

Following this logic, the three elements of the received doctrine of providence (*conservatio, concursus,* and *gubernatio*) might best be understood not as three separate actions or activities of God but as three aspects of the one providential action or activity: the *conservatio* from the Father, the *concursus* in the Spirit, and the *directio* through the Son. God provides "triunely," we might say, in everything that goes on, in a threefold action whose elements may, for the sake of discussion, be abstracted and identified as sustaining, concurring, and directing—even though none of the three is ever present without the others, and none of them, by itself, amounts to an action. Every action of God in creaturely events, every specifiable instance of God's providing, involves these three elements simultaneously.[13]

Now, how might this understanding bear on the treatment of some current difficulties with the notion of God's acting?

It is commonly asserted in Christian formulations of the doctrine of providence that in most, if not all, instances of God's providing, God acts in and through creaturely reality—using "secondary causes," as the philosophical idiom of much classical theology would have it put. (We shall have to deal with the subject of "extraordinary providence" later on, and to confront the question of whether it is ever an exception to this rule.[14]) That is to say, God acts in events that are also

---

12. Gregory of Nyssa, "On Not Three Gods," in *Christology of the Later Fathers*, ed. Edward Rochie Hardy (Philadelphia: Westminster Press, 1954), 261–62. I have amended "in the Father" to "from the Father," and "by the Holy Spirit" to "in the Holy Spirit," to bring the three prepositions into closer harmony with Gregory's *ek, dia,* and *en*. See *Gregorii Nysseni Opera Dogmatica Minora*, part 1, ed. Frederick Mueller (Leiden: E. J. Brill, 1958), 47–48. Although the point about the oneness of divine action is brought out well in the passage quoted, Gregory's portrayal of the relations among the three in such action is sometimes more "linear" (and implicitly hierarchical) than is that of Athanasius or Gregory of Nazianzus, in which these prepositions likewise figure prominently. Sarah Coakley discussed this tension in her 1992 Hulsean Lectures at Cambridge.

13. This logic is obscured or implicitly denied by Quenstedt and other Protestant orthodox writers when they define each of these three aspects as "the action by which God . . . ," giving rise to the impression that sustaining is one action, concurring another, and directing a third.

14. Quenstedt thought it could be. In distinguishing extraordinary from ordinary providence, he wrote, "*Providence* is *extraordinary* when God operates either without means, or

understandable and explicable as acts or events on the creaturely plane: seedtime and harvest, the healing of a physical injury, a political revolution (or the prevention thereof), a word of encouragement from a friend, and so on. An interesting thing about such occurrences is that they (or certain features of them) may be ascribed to God and described as God's acts, while at the same time being fully amenable to description and explanation in nontheological terms. The ascription to God and the explanation on the creaturely plane need not be rivals, unless the advocate of one or the other wishes to assert that this account rules out the alternative: that its being God's act is the only possible explanation for its having happened, or that it can't be God's act because there are perfectly good ways of accounting for it in terms of human agency or natural processes. Such an assertion, however, is best seen as a category mistake. Ascribing an occurrence to God is not a substitute for a "natural" explanation for it or vice versa. The two do different sorts of work in different contexts.[15]

Christian theologians have long been reasonably clear about this in principle, although in practice there have been crucial episodes in which the investigation of the natural causes of natural and human events has been regarded as a threat to Christian doctrine and piety, and vice versa.[16] Certainly to pursue scientific investigation is at least implicitly to deny that a given theological understanding of events has answered all the questions that might legitimately be asked about them. It need not be to deny the adequacy of a theological understanding for its own purposes, nor even to deny the pertinence of theological to scientific understanding (or the other way around).

In recent discussion of the intelligibility of talk about divine

---

beyond and above means, or contrary to means and their nature, or, what is the same, above and beyond the order instituted by Himself, *e.g.*, Ex. 34:28; 1 Kings 19:8; Is. 38:8; 2 Kings 6:6, etc. (all miracles are effects of the extraordinary providence of God). *Providence* is *ordinary* where God carries on His works through ordinary means, viz., through the established and accustomed course of nature" (Quenstedt, *Theologia,* 1:535). The translation is from Heinrich Schmid, *The Doctrinal Theology of the Evangelical Lutheran Church*, 3rd ed., trans. Charles A. Hay and Henry E. Jacobs (Minneapolis: Augsburg Publishing House, 1961), 193.

15. For a fuller account of this distinction, see Charles M. Wood, "The Events In Which God Acts," *An Invitation to Theological Study* (Valley Forge, PA: Trinity Press International, 1994), 90–97.

16. For an account of one such episode, see Margo Todd, "Providence, Chance, and the New Science in Early Stuart Cambridge," *Historical Journal* 29 (1986): 697–711.

action, this understanding of the basic compatibility of the two sorts of discourse—discourse in which events are described in terms of God's action in them and discourse describing events without reference to God—has been called into question on two counts.[17] According to this common critique, ascribing such an occurrence to God, or describing it as God's act, seems arbitrary unless, first, some sense can be given to the notion of God's contributing decisively (if not exclusively) to the realization of the state of affairs involved in the act's description, and second, some way can be found to identify God's intention with the realization of the state of affairs. (Recalling Morris Weitz, we might for the moment think of these two as the "sufficient conditions" for at least some talk of God's providential activity.) But the strength of the "compatibilist" understanding appears to be its weakness precisely when it comes to the satisfaction of these two conditions. If an event is fully explicable in natural (nontheological) terms—that is, if we can account perfectly well for its coming about without reference to God—what sense does it make to assert or imply that God has contributed decisively to its realization? And likewise, if events are fully explicable in natural terms, what warrant can there be for associating certain events, certain features of events, or even events in general with the divine intention?[18]

The grammar of the doctrine of providence suggests a way of meeting these conditions and thus dealing with these questions. It also points to some of the limits Christians ought to observe in ascribing particular happenings to God. Let us see how this is.

The doctrine of the divine *conservatio* points to the fact that in everything that goes on, God is sustaining creation, upholding the

17. These criticisms may be found, in somewhat different forms, in the following: Mats J. Hansson, *Understanding an Act of God: An Essay in Philosophical Theology* (Uppsala: Uppsala University, 1991), esp. chaps. 3 and 7; Maurice Wiles, *God's Action in the World* (London: SCM Press, 1986), esp. chap. 5; and Thomas F. Tracy, "Narrative Theology and the Acts of God," in *Divine Action: Studies Inspired by the Philosophical Theology of Austin Farrer*, ed. Brian Hebblethwaite and Edward Henderson (Edinburgh: T. & T. Clark, 1990), 173–96. They have been addressed in a way that I have found very helpful by Vincent Brümmer, "Farrer, Wiles, and the Causal Joint," *Modern Theology* 8 (1992): 1–14, now reprinted as chap. 5 of his *Speaking of a Personal God* (Cambridge: Cambridge University Press, 1992).

18. We might say that the first challenge is to the legitimacy of theological talk about the "how" of an occurrence, and the second is to the legitimacy of such talk about the "why" of it.

given conditions of creaturely existence. This divine upholding is frequently designated "continuing creation" (*creatio continuata*) as a way of indicating that it is simply the continuing actuality of the primordial act of creation. Christopher Morse has suggested that if creation is analogous to the making of a promise, *conservatio* is analogous to keeping the promise.[19] It is not a matter of repeating the promise, or continually making new promises, but of maintaining the reality and the relationship inaugurated by the original promise. *Conservatio* is a reminder within the doctrine of providence of the radical dependence on God of everything that is and everything that goes on. It is likewise a reminder of the God-given reality, coherence, and integrity of all that is.

It is in this connection that a serious question needs to be raised about the meaning of "extraordinary providence." The older Protestant theology and a good deal of the more recent have asserted that although God ordinarily works in and through creaturely "means," God is also free to disregard these and to work contrary to or without them. But is such an assertion consistent with the doctrine of the divine *conservatio*, or with the doctrine of creation to which it points? It is possible to grant that God may act in unexpected ways, through occurrences that depart from the normal course of things, without claiming that God may act without or contrary to creaturely means as such. A theology that wishes to guard God's absolute power by affirmations of this sort may be in danger of slighting the implications of the covenant promise made in creation and maintained in God's providence.[20]

The theme of *conservatio* supplies part of the answer of the doctrine of providence to the question as to how God might be thought to contribute to what goes on, but by itself it does not yet meet the first of our conditions for meaningful speech of God's activity in what

---

19. Christopher Morse, *Not Every Spirit: A Dogmatics of Christian Disbelief* (Valley Forge, PA: Trinity Press International, 1994), 217.

20. Christopher Morse questions this supposition on other (but closely related) doctrinal grounds: "In the words of the Westminster Confession of 1647: 'God, in his ordinary providence, maketh use of means, yet is free to work without, above, and against them, at his pleasure.' There is at this point disagreement in Christian theology over whether it is coherent with faith in the Incarnation to speak of God providing for creation, as the Westminster Confession puts it, 'without' any creaturely means" (*Not Every Spirit*, 220).

goes on. The theme of the divine *concursus* takes us further toward the goal, for it speaks not only of God's upholding the conditions within which everything that happens happens, but also of God's direct or immediate involvement in everything that happens. If *conservatio* says that all creatures are upheld in their existence and in their activities by the God from whom they ultimately derive,[21] *concursus* says that God is so intimately involved in those activities as to *enact* them simultaneously with the creatures themselves. Creaturely existence and activity is not only *from* God but *in* God, as indicated by what is perhaps the favorite biblical text invoked in the discussion of this doctrine, Acts 17:28: "'For "In him we live and move and have our being."'"[22] But here, some important conceptual distinctions and qualifications need to be observed.

A fairly standard depiction of the divine concurrence (e.g., in J. A. Quenstedt) indicates that it is that aspect of God's providing whereby God "gently influences" (*suaviter influit*) the actions and doings of creatures by an "inflowing" (*influxus*) of the divine presence and power, fitting to the circumstances of each creature and occasion, so that the creature's activity is at the same time the divine activity.[23] The language of inflowing, indwelling, and immediate divine presence brings to mind the particular association of the divine *concursus* with the Holy Spirit. Quenstedt observes that this theme "coincides" in its own way with the theme of the divine omnipresence, but with the important proviso that this omnipresence is to be understood in a biblical and not a philosophical sense (not *sensu philosophico*, but *sensu & stylo Biblico*). The texts he

---

21. "Conservatio est *actus divinae providentiae, quo Deus res omnes a se creatas in suo esse, h. e. in sua natura & naturalibus proprietatibus & viribus, quas in prima sui productione acceperunt, conservat, quousque vult*" (Quenstedt, *Theologia*, 1:531).

22. Phillip Cary notes the compatibility, in the Areopagus speech, of the language of God's "transcendence" and God's "immanence"—indeed, the difficulty of distinguishing them at times—and suggests that this feature of early Christian talk about God (through the Cappadocians and on to John of Damascus) supports the thesis of Kathryn Tanner that Christian discourse operates rightly on a principle of "non-contrastive transcendence." See Cary, "On Behalf of Classical Trinitarianism," 400–401, and Kathryn Tanner, *God and Creation in Christian Theology* (Oxford: Basil Blackwell, 1988), esp. chap. 2.

23. "Concursus est *actus providentiae divinae, quo Deus influxu generali in actiones & effectus causarum secondarum, qua tales, se ipso immediate & simul cum eis & juxta indigentiam & exigentiam uniuscujusque suaviter influit*" (Quenstedt, *Theologia*, 1:531).

adduces here (e.g., Gen. 1:2, Ps. 137:7) are mainly (though not exclusively) references to the presence and activity of the Spirit.[24] There is, according to this doctrine, no creaturely doing that does not involve a divine doing. God is not merely the medium of our existence, like the water in a fishbowl in which the fish live and move and have their being. Rather, our living is a participation in the divine life; our moving, a participation in the divine moving. The formulators of the classical doctrine worked to preserve this startling intimacy and to guard against both a sheer identification of God and creature and a stark separation between them. The language they used, although affected by the then-current (mainly Aristotelian) philosophical vocabulary, is in some ways reminiscent of the ancient christological settlement:

> God not only gives and preserves to second causes the power to act
> . . . but immediately influences the action and effect of the creature,
> so that the same effect is produced not by God alone, nor by the
> creature alone, nor partly by God and partly by the creature, but *at
> the same time by God and the creature*, as one and the same total
> efficiency, viz., by God as the universal and first cause, and by the
> creature as the particular and second cause.[25]

In this account, Quenstedt avoids one problem that has sometimes dogged the doctrine of concurrence and the notion of divine activity generally. He does not say, as some of his colleagues did, that "one and the same *act*" is performed by both God and the creature(s) simultaneously. He says, rather, that "one and the same *effect*" (or "one and the same doing" perhaps: *idem effectus, una eademque efficientia*) is brought about simultaneously by both. The idea of two agents performing the identical act is widely (and in my judgment rightly) regarded as incoherent, because act description is at least implicitly always "agent-involving." An act is always *someone's* act,

---

24. Ibid., 1:532.

25. "De Concursu causae primae cum secundis observandum I. quod Deus non solum vim agendi det causis secundis & eam conservet . . . sed quod immediate influat in actionem & effectum creaturae, ita ut idem effectus non a solo Deo, nec a sola creatura, nec partim a Deo, partim a creatura, sed una eademque efficientia totali simul a Deo & creatura producatur, a Deo videl. ut *causa universali & prima*, a creatura, ut *particulari & secunda*" (Ibid., 1:531). The translation quoted is from Schmid, *Doctrinal Theology*, 180.

even if the agent is, at the moment, unknown. Your act of *x*-ing (singing, say) cannot be simultaneously my act of *x*-ing. If you and I are *x*-ing at the same time, or even if we are *x*-ing together, there are still two acts of *x*-ing involved—unless it is really a joint act to which we are each making a (specifiable) contribution. (In that case, what each of us is doing as his or her contribution is more justly regarded as his or her own individual act.) Our performing "one and the same act" entails that we are identical, that is, that there is no "we" but a single agent. If "double agency" is taken in this way, it is assuredly a dead end, at least for anyone who holds that God and creation are distinct realities.

The doctrine of concurrence guards the distinction between God and creatures in other ways even while it stresses the intimacy of their relation. One of these is adumbrated in Quenstedt's observation that God is the *universal* cause, and creatures, *particular* causes. The distinction between God and creatures has in part to do with the latter's particularity, their being located spatially and temporally, and bounded internally (so to speak) by their own identities and externally by their fellow creatures. Creation is finite and complex. It is also marked by a God-given freedom (or something analogous to freedom at lower levels of complexity, if the term "freedom" is reserved for its higher manifestations). If creation is indeed distinct from God and not merely an extension of God's own being, creaturely being and doing cannot be entirely determined by God but must in part be self-determined. That is, each creature's nature and activity are determined in part by itself and by other creatures, as well as by God.[26] Thus particular creatures have distinctive contributions to make to the way God's will or intention is realized in given situations. With the divine concurrence, creatures may act freely in any of various ways that might be seen to constitute enactments of God's will. The idea that genuine creaturely action in which God concurs must follow one predetermined path is not an implication of the doctrine of the divine concurrence; rather, that doctrine would seem to protect creatures' freedom to realize themselves in actions in which they themselves make a genuine difference.

---

26. See William A. Christian, "God and the World," *Journal of Religion* 28 (1948): 255–62.

The distinction between God and creatures is maintained by this doctrine in another way as well. According to a principle that Quenstedt borrows from his predecessors that goes back at least to Aquinas, God concurs in creaturely doings but not in what we might call creaturely "undoings."[27] All genuine creaturely action is realized only through the divine concurrence. But creatures are also capable (in a strange sense of "capable") of failure. With the finitude, particularity, and complexity of creation comes the possibility of several sorts of undoing. First, the plurality of creatures brings with it the possibility and virtual inevitability of conflict and thus the frustration of some creatures' aims for the sake of the fulfillment of the aims of others. God may concur in the activities of each of a number of creatures in a given situation, even when these activities will bring the creatures into conflict and the success of some in their doings will mean the failure or destruction of others. Second, creatures may fail in their actions of their own accord and not only because of resistance or opposition from without. "Fault" is a constant possibility in creaturehood. Here we must distinguish between what we may call natural failings, due to inherent weakness or simply to the spatiotemporal limitations of a given sort of creatureliness (aging, for example), and what we might call moral fault, in which something like refusal or "willful undoing" is always a component. All three of these—the failures induced by creaturely conflict, natural failings, and moral fault—are embraced by the principle that God concurs in the effect (the "doing") of the creature but not in the defect (the "undoing"). We might say that all genuine creaturely action is enabled by the divine concurrence, accomplished in the Holy Spirit (to follow Gregory's usage), while those apparent actions that manifest creaturely fault are not proper actions at all but disactions, undoings.

We have in the developed concept of concurrence, then, the recognition that God relates in different ways to different creaturely goings-on: concurring in the creatures' genuine activity but not concurring in creaturely undoing. But given that most if not all creaturely situations involve a mixture of genuine activity, the frustration of such activity, and one if not both sorts of creaturely fault, how are we to

---

understand more particularly how God is related to all this: what is God doing, how is God acting, in a given situation? The third component of the inherited doctrine of providence, the doctrine of the divine governance, offers some resources for our consideration here. (Its particular categories may not be found entirely adequate, but they are suggestive.) This aspect of the doctrine of providence establishes the principle that God's intentions are not simply to be read off what comes to pass. God is providing *in* everything that goes on but relates differently to different elements of what is occurring: empowering creaturely existence and action, allowing creaturely conflict and failing, opposing the consequences of creaturely undoing, and working in and with each situation toward new possibilities for the fulfillment of creation's purpose.

Following again the summation of Quenstedt, the doctrine of the divine governance is that aspect of the doctrine of providence having to do with God's "ordering" of creaturely activities toward God's own purposes.[28] Four sorts of ordering are conventionally distinguished: permission, hindrance, direction, and determination. *Permissio* signifies God's willing allowance of creaturely fault; *impeditio*, God's obstruction of evil purposes; *directio*, God's channelling the consequences of creaturely decisions, whether good or ill, in accordance with God's own purposes; and *determinatio*, the limits that God has appointed to creaturely "powers, actions, and passions" that they may not transcend.[29]

The logic of this fourfold distinction is not particularly clear (at least to my mind), and there are serious problems in the conventional explication of each of the terms. Here even more than elsewhere the traditional doctrine seems to have departed from the direction an appropriately Trinitarian or christologically oriented doctrine might have gone. It is difficult, on the basis of this traditional categorization, not to think of God's governance or ordering of creaturely affairs as

---

28. "Tertius divinae providentiae *actus* est Gubernatio, qua *Deus omnes & singulas creaturas suas in viribus, actionibus & passionibus suis decenter ordinat, ad Creatoris gloriam, & universi hujus bonum, ac piorum imprimis salutem*" (Ibid., 1:533). Quenstedt is careful to note that such government does not violate the natures of either "natural" or "free" creatures, i.e., it respects both natural processes and moral agency.

29. See Ibid., 1:534, for an only slightly fuller treatment of these elements.

a kind of manipulation, a continual intervention in the creaturely realm on the part of a distant and unaffected deity who "permits" evil and suffering (although certainly capable of preventing them), encourages or interferes with creaturely activity at will, and generally arranges things to come out according to the divine plan. The doctrine of the divine governance might be radically transformed if it were seriously considered that it is "through the Son" (as it is "from the Father" and "in the Spirit") that God's providing activity proceeds. Trinitarian talk about God's ordering of creaturely affairs must take its bearings decisively from what is disclosed of God's manner of working in Jesus Christ.

In this connection, Thomas F. Torrance recalls a principle of Hilary of Poitiers. Hilary, notes Torrance,

> insists that everything we actually think and say of God must be constrained and controlled within the bounds of the revelation of the Father in and through the incarnate Son. This is a revelation of God's almightiness that conflicts with the idea of limitless arbitrary power which we generate out of our this worldly experiences, make infinite, and attribute to God, for the divine power manifest in Jesus Christ is of an altogether different kind. It is not in terms of what *we* think God *can do*, but in terms of what God *has done and continues to do* in Jesus Christ that we may understand something of what divine almightiness really is.[30]

Amplifying the same insight as to the necessity of connecting Trinitarian and christological reflection on this issue, D. M. MacKinnon writes, "It is a weakness of the western Trinitarian tradition so to conceive and so to stress the unity of God that the whole theology of the divine attributes tends to be treated independently of the treatise of the divine tri-unity, and the unity of God itself regarded as conceivable independently of the tri-unity through which it is realized." He goes on to say that we must learn to define the power of God in terms of the hands "stretched in weakness," and not over against that weakness. "We are not passing through the hour of a temporary

---

30. Thomas F. Torrance, *The Trinitarian Faith: The Evangelical Theology of the Ancient Catholic Church* (Edinburgh: T. & T. Clark, 1988), 82. The reference is to Hilary, *De Trin*, 3:1–5.

eclipse of the divine sovereignty where we are concerned," MacKinnon maintains. "We are witnessing its supreme assertion in the setting of a deeply estranged world, an assertion that discloses its very
substance, its arcane ground. Our images of the divine are always per-
ilously suffused with anthropomorphic suggestions of a consummate
mastery of the world."[31]

If one took these admonitions seriously, what would an account of
God's ordering or governing look like? The next chapter will pursue
this question. But while the terms are fresh in mind, let us consider
for a moment how such an approach might lead to a reconception of
the traditional four elements of the divine *gubernatio*—assuming for
the moment that there is reason to retain this scheme. The notion of
"permission" (*permissio*) is closely related to the theme of *conservatio*: In covenant faithfulness, God maintains the conditions that allow
creaturely undoing as well as creaturely flourishing. The latter cannot be had without the possibility of the former. Although God does
not concur in creaturely fault, as the author and sustainer of creation
God must be said in some sense to allow it. This admission, however,
is misleading unless it is also stressed that God *suffers* creaturely fault
and its consequences, not simply in the weaker, archaic sense of "suffering" but in the sense represented by the prophetic tradition (e.g.,
Hosea) and by the cross.[32] The notion of hindrance (*impeditio*) might
be shown to have to do with God's unwavering opposition to creaturely destruction, God's steadfast will for creation's own good.
Direction (*directio*) might be taken to signify God's ability to take up
creaturely activity, both good and ill, into God's ongoing purposes.
And the theme of determination (*determinatio*), referring to the
divine limitations appointed to all creaturely activity and its consequences, might also be given a more evangelical sense: creatures,
thank God, do not have the last word as to what their being and doing
will amount to. In some such way, I believe, the inherited doctrine of

31. D. M. MacKinnon, "The Relation of the Doctrines of the Incarnation and the Trinity,"
Creation, Christ and Culture: Essays in Honour of T. F. Torrance, ed. Richard W. A. McKin-
ney (Edinburgh: T. & T. Clark, 1976), 99.

32. The Protestant orthodox writers did not appear to give much attention to the question of
whether the possibility of God's *not* allowing creaturely fault is at all consistent either with
God's nature or with the fundamental conditions for their being a creation at all. More recent
writers from a variety of perspectives have taken up these questions.

the divine governance would need to be reconceived. In the long run, however, it might be better to replace it with a more adequate conceptualization than to retain the present categories.

To summarize this exploration of the Trinitarian grammar of the doctrine of providence: *Conservatio* affirms the ultimate grounding of what goes on in God's sustaining of creaturely being and doing. *Concursus* affirms that all genuine creaturely activity is simultaneously describable as God's activity, so that whatever is not so describable has the (perhaps ontologically problematic) status of a disaction or undoing. *Gubernatio* affirms that all creaturely occurrence—all doing and undoing—receives its specific intelligibility, its identity and meaning, from the way it is received by God and dealt with by God, and it finds its ultimate end in God. God is thus the ultimate ground, context, and end of what goes on; to understand theologically any particular part of what goes on is a matter of seeing it in the context of this threefold providing. God's providing is one triune activity. Its aspects may be distinguished as *conservatio, concursus*, and *gubernatio* so as to bring out more explicitly what it means to say that God is acting "triunely" in this providing, as the one from whom, in whom, and to whom all creation lives.

Chapter 5

The One with Whom We Have to Do

*He ministers indeed to all our good but all our good is other
than we thought.*
　　—*H. Richard Niebuhr,* The Meaning of Revelation[1]

An Instance of Doctrine

In December 1942, the Federal Council of the Churches of Christ in
America established a commission to study "The Relation of the
Church to the War in the Light of the Christian Faith" and to produce
a report on the subject for the guidance of its member churches. The
commission's initial membership, a roster including some of the most
distinguished theologians in North America, was appointed in March
1943, with Professor Robert Lowry Calhoun of Yale as its chair. The
body soon became known as the "Calhoun Commission." It held four
plenary sessions and a number of subsection meetings during 1943
and 1944, and issued its report in November 1944.[2] The report was

---

1. H. Richard Niebuhr, *The Meaning of Revelation* (New York: Macmillan Co., 1941), 191.

2. *The Relation of the Church to the War in the Light of the Christian Faith* (New York: Federal Council of the Churches of Christ in America, 1944). Subsequent parenthetical page references in this chapter are to this publication. A slightly abridged version of the report is available in *War in the Twentieth Century*, ed. Richard B. Miller (Louisville, KY: Westminster/John Knox Press, 1992), 71–124. The central section is reproduced in its entirety in *Creeds of the Churches*, ed. John Leith (Louisville, KY: John Knox Press, 1982), 522–54.

The members of the commission, as listed at the conclusion of the report, were as follows: Edwin E. Aubrey, Roland H. Bainton, John C. Bennett, Conrad J. I. Bergendoff, B. Harvie Branscomb, Frank H. Caldwell, Robert Lowry Calhoun, Angus Dun, Nels F. S. Ferré, Robert

greeted, warmly commended, disseminated, and briefly discussed in the Protestant press; but by the time of its release the attention of both church and nation had already turned in anticipation to other, "postwar" issues—among them "A Just and Durable Peace" (the title and topic of another Federal Council study then underway)—and the reflection embodied in the Calhoun Commission report has received scant attention since.

This neglect, though understandable, is regrettable, not least because the report contains what I believe to be the most valuable brief articulation of the Christian doctrine of providence produced during the past century. Its value derives from the circumstances of its production and its character as a doctrinal act, as well as from its content. While the content will be the main focus of our attention in this chapter, these other two features should not be overlooked in an estimate of the doctrinal importance of this commission's work.

Two facts in particular are significant regarding the circumstances of the report's production, and both are suggested by an editorial comment in *The Christian Century*: "[T]he churches, through their Federal Council, have turned to their theologians for light on a problem which sorely distresses them."[3] First, although the commission was not a church council with the authority to promulgate official doctrine, it was in some sense a churchly body: it was a group of the churches' thinkers, drawn from various Protestant traditions, deliberating and giving counsel to the churches at their request. The commission spoke *to* the churches, not *for* them; but it spoke corporately and from within. Second, it was created to address a serious practical concern and to provide doctrinal resources that would enable the churches to respond to that concern more faithfully and effectively. Here, as at other important junctures in Christian history, doctrinal exploration was provoked, informed, and tested by a pressing need.

As to the character of the report as an act of teaching, two facts

---

E. Fitch, Theodore M. Greene, Georgia E. Harkness, Walter M. Horton, John Knox, Umphrey Lee, John A. Mackay, Benjamin E. Mays, John T. McNeill, H. Richard Niebuhr, Reinhold Niebuhr, William Pauck, Douglas V. Steere, Ernest Fremont Tittle, Henry P. Van Dusen, Theodore O. Wedel, and Alexander C. Zabriskie.

3. Unsigned editorial, "The Theologians' Report," *The Christian Century* 61, no. 49 (December 6, 1944), 1407.

again stand out. First, the report is written so as to invite rather than to discourage its readers' own constructive engagement and reflection. The structure and rhetoric of the report are suited to lead the reader into a deep consideration of the issues and thus to the acquisition of a fuller understanding both of the Christian faith and of the situation with which it is being confronted, without forcing the adoption of one particular view or course of action. Second, the report uses a kind of Christian vernacular language that transcends many denominational boundaries, is accessible to the common reader, and addresses the heart as well as the mind. In this, despite many obvious differences, the report resembles the more memorable and successful popular doctrinal treatises of the seventeenth century. It aims not merely to inform but also to capacitate the reader. It engages the affections, enabling the doctrinal content to take root. It requires the reader's involvement at several levels, and it repays the attention and effort it requires.[4]

The report is divided into three sections. An initial "diagnostic" section offers an analysis of the situation to which the commission is responding. A "doctrinal" section then develops "a statement of those primary Christian affirmations that seem to us normative for any attempt to deal with the problems of the Church in war-time." The concluding "practical" section considers some appropriate Christian responses to the situation in light of those affirmations (8–9). The central, doctrinal section is, in effect, a constructive restatement of the doctrine of providence. The word "providence" appears only rarely in the document, perhaps because its authors sensed that its use would be more problematic than helpful. The traditional terminology of the doctrine is likewise scarce, but the substance is unmistakable.

Two basic methodological decisions are largely responsible for the document's material importance as a contribution to Christian

---

4. "It does not present us with cut-and-dried answers to the questions raised. . . . No reader of the report could wish a mere *ipsi dixit* from this commission. What the church needs and every Christian must desire is to see the problem of war in the large context of the Christian faith. This the commission has done for us. . . . Yet it must not be inferred that the report is difficult reading, and that only those with special intellectual equipment can follow it. Any thoughtful layman or minister can read it if he brings to it a *patient* mind" ("The Theologians' Report," 1408).

reflection on this doctrine. The first is a decision to ground its doctrinal affirmations primarily in "the revelation of God in Jesus Christ"
(22), and thus to attempt a specifically *Christian* understanding of
how God is related to what is going on. The second is a decision to
follow a Trinitarian "grammar" in developing these affirmations
(29–43) and to allow that grammar itself to be christologically governed in both form and content. There are, to be sure, certain problems and limitations in the execution of these decisions. Some of
these problems and limitations are perhaps inherent in the theological situation of mid-twentieth-century America, and others might be
traced to features of the particular minds at work on this commission
and to their interaction. The positive contributions, however, far out-
weigh the difficulties.

My aim here is to offer both an exposition and a constructive critique of the doctrine of providence presented in this report. The intervening years have not diminished its usefulness; if anything, they
have intensified it. Christian understanding of God's providence in
the twenty-first century might be greatly advanced by the thoughtful
reception of this gift from our relatively recent past.

The report as it stands is the common work of the full commission.
It was shaped by its discussions as well as by a number of authorial
and editorial hands, and it was published as its corporate utterance.
Those acquainted with the thought and writings of individual members of the commission may discern (or, at least, suspect) their distinctive contributions at various points. H. Richard Niebuhr's
influence seems to many to pervade both the substance and the idiom
of the report and to be especially strong in the central section. Niebuhr
chaired the subdivision of the commission that was responsible for
drafting this section and wrote a preliminary study as a basis for their
discussion.[5] He had been at work for some time on subjects highly
pertinent to the commission's reflections. Much in the report's treatment of revelation is reminiscent of Niebuhr's book *The Meaning of
Revelation*, published in 1941 and destined to become a classic of

---

5. See "A Christian Interpretation of War" in H. Richard Niebuhr, *Theology, History, and
Culture: Major Unpublished Writings*, ed. William Stacy Johnson (New Haven, CT: Yale University Press, 1996), 159–73. Illness prevented Niebuhr from being involved in the final stages
of the commission's work.

twentieth-century theology. Other themes in the report, and especially its treatments of judgment and of the cross, are explored more
directly in a set of articles by Niebuhr published in *The Christian
Century* in 1942 and 1943, the last of these just as the commission
was getting underway.[6] The influence was not all in one direction,
however. The commission's work was, to a large extent, the continuation of a theological conversation among its members that had been
going on for many years, and Niebuhr, like others involved, candidly
and gratefully acknowledged the help his own thinking had received
from other participants in this ongoing collaboration.[7]

The Revelatory Occasion

The central, doctrinal section of the report begins with this assertion,
under the heading of "Grounds of a Christian Understanding of the
War": *"The primary ground for a distinctive Christian understanding of any situation is the revelation of God in Jesus Christ"* (22).
The report affirms that there have been "continuing revelations of
God through the work of the Holy Spirit" not only in the history
recorded in Hebrew and Christian Scriptures and in subsequent
Christian experience but throughout "the whole world of nature and
man." As Christians see it, however, the "crucial disclosure" is in

---

6. H. Richard Niebuhr, "War as the Judgment of God," *The Christian Century* 59 (May 3,
1942): 630–33; "Is God in the War?" *The Christian Century* 59 (August 5, 1942): 953–55; "War
as Crucifixion," *The Christian Century* 60 (April 28, 1943): 513–15. These "war articles" are
reprinted in *War in the Twentieth Century*, ed. Richard B. Miller (see note 2 above); the first
and third are also reproduced in a booklet, *War as Crucifixion: Essays on Peace, Violence, and
"Just War,"* ed. John Buchanan and David Heim (Chicago: Christian Century Press, 2002),
17–29. In "H. Richard Niebuhr's War Articles: A Transvaluation of Value," *Journal of Religion*
58 (1998), Richard B. Miller remarks that the Calhoun Commission report "clearly and indeli-
bly bears Niebuhr's signature" (261).

7. See, for example, the preface to Niebuhr, *The Meaning of Revelation.* Eighteen of the
twenty-six signers of the Calhoun Commission report were members of the Yale-based Theological Discussion Group, which had held conferences twice a year since its founding in 1934.
About half of the Calhoun group were members of the American Theological Society, established earlier in the century and meeting annually to discuss work in progress. Some had col-
laborated on other projects or were linked by other ecclesial or academic affiliations. On these
interrelated groups, see Heather A. Warren, *Theologians of a New World Order: Reinhold
Niebuhr and the Christian Realists 1920–1948* (New York: Oxford University Press, 1997), esp.
61–63 and 110–112.

Jesus Christ, "from whose light these other areas derive new meaning" (22–23).

"Revelation of God in Jesus Christ takes place whenever and wherever human persons find themselves effectively confronted, through the Gospel record or some spoken word, through personal contact or social heritage, inside or outside the institutional Church, by the person Jesus of Nazareth as an embodiment of unqualified moral judgment and regenerating power, 'God's power and God's wisdom'" (23). Normally, the encounter with Jesus Christ is mediated by a written record (the New Testament) and a living community (the church) working in conjunction. The confrontation leads to "a personal reorientation . . . a basic response of the whole self" (24) that then affects one's understanding of everything else. Everything in our experience is thus to be interpreted or reinterpreted in light of this revelatory occasion. A key principle for a Christian understanding not only of the war but of everything that goes on emerges from this concept of revelation: *The Christian comes to each event in his or mankind's history with the confidence that he is dealing with something that contains divine meaning, that is intelligible, if not in every detail yet in essence, in terms of the faithful working of God* (25).

The report acknowledges that our apprehension of the revelation of God in Jesus Christ is always partial and conditioned. The differences in our experience and interests lead to differences of understanding. Further, our discernment of God's working in all events in light of the revelatory event is always subject to error (27). An awareness of the fallibility and partiality of our grasp of things drives us continually to seek correction and amplification of our insights in community, with the guidance of the Holy Spirit (28–29).

Two points in this treatment of revelation deserve particular emphasis. One is the concept of the revelatory event as the event in whose light we can see the significance of other events. In *The Meaning of Revelation*, Niebuhr quotes a sentence from Alfred North Whitehead's *Religion in the Making* and adds a comment. Whitehead wrote, "Rational religion appeals to the direct intuition of special occasions, and to the elucidatory power of its concepts for all occasions." Niebuhr comments, "The special occasion to which we appeal in the Christian church is called Jesus Christ, in whom we see the righteousness of God, his power and wisdom. But from that special occasion we also derive the concepts which make possible the elucidation of all the events in our history. Revelation means this intelligible event which makes all other events intelligible."[8] This is essentially the position of the Calhoun report. A little later in his account, Niebuhr writes, "The revelatory moment is revelatory because it is rational, because it makes the understanding of order and meaning in personal history possible. Through it a pattern of dramatic unity becomes apparent with the aid of which the heart can understand what has happened, is happening and will happen to selves in their community."[9]

The second point, closely linked to this, is that the response to revelation involves a radical reorientation of the self. The report amplifies this converting or transforming power of the revelatory encounter: under its impact, "both knowledge and will proceed upon lines not open before, yet so related to the past life and the persisting nature of the believer that he finds in his new orientation a powerful expansion and correction of all that he has been. Through faith, as through love, he becomes a new person, in whom new insights and energies come to life, though never in simple escape from the old self nor from essential human limitations" (25).

The revelatory encounter with God in Christ provokes a deep-going change. It is not just that we see different things, things that we had not seen before; rather, we see all things differently. We see with new eyes, or—less metaphorically put—we understand with different conceptual equipment.[10] In the closing paragraphs of *The Meaning of Revelation*, Niebuhr movingly describes the "transvaluation of values" this revelatory experience elicits:

So we must begin to rethink all our definitions of deity and convert all our worship and our prayers. . . . The self we loved is not the self God loves, the neighbors we did not prize are his treasures, the truth we ignored is the truth he maintains, the justice which we

8. Niebuhr, *The Meaning of Revelation*, 93.

9. Ibid., 109–10.

10. Recall the discussion of concepts in chap. 1, 6ff. The Brazilian theologian Clodovis Boff describes this outcome of the revelatory encounter as the acquisition of a "hermeneutical competency" or "hermeneutical *habitus*," when Christians learn from Scripture how to read reality differently. Clodovis Boff, *Theology and Praxis: Epistemological Foundations*, trans. Robert R. Barr (Maryknoll, NY: Orbis Books, 1987), chap. 8.

sought because it was our own is not the justice that his love desires. The righteousness he demands and gives is not our righteousness but greater and different. . . . He ministers indeed to all our good but all our good is other than we thought.[11]

The importance of this point for a Christian doctrine of providence should not be underestimated. It is the *character* of the transformation, and not merely the fact of one, that is crucial to grasp. The Stoicism that informs the traditional doctrine of providence emphasized a kind of conversion—from the ordinary cares of life to *apatheia*—that bears a formal resemblance to what Niebuhr is here describing. The resemblance is most apparent in what might be called the negative moment of conversion: the demand for a renunciation. The same is evident in Boethius's synthesis of Stoicism with other elements of the classical tradition. The point held in common here is that inappropriate attachments are preventing the realization of human purpose. Where these early accounts and a more genuinely Christian perspective most decisively diverge is in the understanding of what we are to be converted *toward*. For Boethius, "true and perfect happiness" consists in the recovery of our true, God-like nature: "self-sufficient, strong, worthy of respect, glorious and joyful."[12] On this view, to participate in the nature of divinity is to be detached, independent, and invulnerable. The consolation offered by doctrines of providence in this tradition is basically the assurance that, despite appearances, God always protects and rewards the good (i.e., the God-like) and punishes the wicked. For the more philosophically sophisticated, such as Boethius, the rewards and punishments are intrinsic.

It was this sort of consolation that led Simone Weil to reject the received notion of providence not simply as non-Christian but as contrary to the gospel.[13] The gospel, for Weil, is not about the securing

---

11. Niebuhr, *The Meaning of Revelation*, 190–91.

12. Boethius, *The Consolation of Philosophy*, trans. Victor Watts (rev. ed.; London: Penguin Books, 1999), 65. The contrast between Boethian and Christian sensibilities is vividly described by Ernst Hoffmann, "Griechiche Philosophie und christliches Dogma bei Boethius," in *Boethius*, ed. Manfred Fuhrmann and Joachim Gruber (Darmstadt: Wissenschaftliche Buchgesellschaft, 1984), 278–85.

13. Simone Weil, *Gravity and Grace*, trans. Emma Crawford and Mario von der Ruhr (London: Routledge, 2002), 13–15.

of the self from harm; it is rather about the gracious possibility of a kind of self-abandonment in love that Weil called "decreation." That term and the concept it represents are somewhat problematic and reflect some unresolved tensions in Weil's thought, but Weil's reflections on the sort of reorientation Christian life involves contain much that is helpful. For her, partaking of the divine nature does not mean achieving invulnerability. It means precisely the opposite. She makes it clear that this conviction is grounded in her understanding of God's self-revelation in Jesus Christ.[14] A similar conviction on this point is reflected in the Calhoun Commission report.

We will need to engage later on in a fuller exploration of the character and significance of this radical reorientation.

A Trinitarian Vision

Both in its overall structure and in the organization and content of its central doctrinal affirmations, the Calhoun Commission report is shaped by a Trinitarian logic. This logic is made most explicit as the report turns from its discussion of the revelatory ground of its understanding of how God is related to what goes on to its explication of the general pattern of the divine activity: "*In this mood, we venture to affirm next our belief that God's relation to the war is defined in broad terms by His essential unitary activity as Creator, Redeemer, Life-Giver.* These are not three activities, but one, as the Father, Son, and Holy Spirit of Christian teaching are not three Gods but one" (29).

Several things are to be noted about this brief affirmation. First, according to the authors' own express commitments, this understanding of the divine activity is derived primarily from what the report calls "the revelation of God in Jesus Christ." It is not an independent insight from some other source but the outworking of what is seen in the light of the revelatory event. Second, the association of creation, redemption, and the giving of life with the Father, the Son, and the Holy Spirit observes the Trinitarian "grammar" outlined in our fourth chapter. These are not three separate acts assigned to three

---

14. Ibid., 32–39.

separate agents. There is, rather, a triunity in all that God does, corresponding to the triunity within God. Creation, redemption, and life giving or "renovation" are three aspects of one divine action (29).

Third, although the document does not use the traditional three providential categories of *conservatio*, *gubernatio*, and *concursus*, its discussion of the three aspects of the one divine action may readily be coordinated with those three terms, in accord with the Trinitarian construal of them that was offered in chapter 4. This coordination, as pursued in the exposition that follows, is intended to overcome the problematic isolation of the doctrine of providence and to exhibit its coinherence with other themes in Christian doctrine.

Under the heading of "God as Creator," the report affirms that "the existence of every situation depends on the creative energy of God's will, put forth not merely in some past moment of time but throughout all time" (29–30). A strong understanding of providence as *creatio continua* is evident here. "From no portion of the existing world is God absent. . . . The presence of God is never static but always active presence, not merely form or law but energy. God is then present, active, creative, in every part of nature and history, and so in this war" (30). Although some traditional writers might have qualms about the report's failure to make a clear distinction between "creation" and "conservation," the substance of what has been said here might be derived from any number of standard treatises on God's sustaining providence.

What immediately follows is not so familiar, however. Having acknowledged the constant, utter dependence of creation on the will and energy of the Creator, the report is next at pains to insist on the God-given reality, integrity, and relative independence of creation, and to spell out some of the crucial implications of that status:

> If there is no event from which God is absent, equally there is no event in which God alone is present. In as far as creation is effective, it brings into existence and maintains in existence subordinate centers and fields of energy that are at once yielding and resistant to the continuing energy of their Creator, as well as embodying attraction and repulsion, partial harmony and partial discord among themselves. (30)

In human history (to which "this comment applies with especial pertinence"), the situation is especially complex: what is going on in human history is always the combined result of God's activity, the action of "natural and impersonal forces," and human decision. *The truth as it seems to us is that the war is neither simply a natural fact nor an act of God nor a sinful choice of man. It is a complex event in which all of these factors are present, and need to be duly recognized*" (31). Though the report is speaking here specifically of the war, the principle is more generally applicable. What happens in war, or in nature and history generally, "is not divinely ordained" (32). It is brought about, rather, by the interplay of divine action and various sorts of creaturely action, in greater or lesser harmony.

The Methodist theologian Georgia Harkness, a member of the commission and a longtime participant in the earlier theological conversations among many of its members, later published her own reflections on providence in a brief book titled simply *The Providence of God*. In it, she proposes a distinction between what happens by God's *power* and what happens according to God's *purpose*. Her distinction here appears to resonate with the commission's account of this first aspect of God's relation to what goes on. She writes,

> If "this is my Father's world," as Christians not only sing but deeply believe, all that happens in nature happens by God's power. But this does *not* mean that everything happens by the specific will and purpose of God. This distinction is crucial. That it is the wise and good purpose of God to create and maintain an orderly world of nature we must believe; this does not obligate us to believe that every event that occurs within it is according to His purpose and therefore to be accounted good.[15]

What she says here of the "world of nature" applies equally, in her judgment (as in the evident judgment of the commission), to the world of human moral agency. God's creative energy sustains and enables everything that happens. Creatures, exercising the power given to them with their existence, may, in their freedom, realize the divine purpose

---

15. Georgia Harkness, *The Providence of God* (Nashville: Abingdon Press, 1960), 90. Harkness was a member of both the American Theological Society and the Theological Discussion Group.

in a great variety of ways, but they may also act in ways that frustrate the divine purpose in a given situation. The report itself puts the matter in more detail, again with specific reference to the wartime situation:

> God, then, acts in the war as the creative ground that continuously keeps the warring world and its members in existence, and enables them to act in accordance with their respective natures or decisions. God does not act as an all-inclusive "One-and-All," nor in any way that excludes or nullifies decision and action by His creatures. Moreover, God does not act as a world Ruler who has willed the outbreak of the war, nor all those specific antecedent conditions that made the war inescapable. Some of these conditions God directly wills, we believe—the freedom and the interdependence of men, the inseparability of moral decisions from natural consequences, and the like. Others are the resultants of natural forces that operate in relatively uniform causal networks, perhaps without complete mechanical fixity but presumably without the foresight or decision characteristic of persons: natural forces that operate, then, often in ways that enhance or destroy values, even perhaps in ways that further or hamper the will of God, but that are not themselves amenable to moral judgment. Some are the personal decisions of men, together with their antecedents and consequences, some personal, others more or less impersonal, but all identified more directly with responsible human action than with the irresponsible forces of extra-human nature, and all involving a crucial factor of human difference from, and often of opposition to, the will of God. (31)[16]

This account of God's relation to what goes on may seem to demote God to the status of one agent among many and to compromise the divine transcendence. This is not necessarily the case. The membership of the Calhoun Commission encompassed a considerable range of theological viewpoints, but nothing in its report is inconsistent with a strong affirmation of the transcendence and sovereignty of God. The report does powerfully challenge certain *views* of God's transcendence and sovereignty—views that were cultivated over long centuries by standard treatises on providence and that dominated early modern theology in general following the seventeenth-

16. Cf. chap. 4 above, 86–87.

century eclipse of the doctrine of the Trinity.[17] It represents an alternative construal, perhaps not fully articulated in the thinking of any individual on the commission, but at least latent in the minds of many. H. Richard Niebuhr, for example, had as strong a sense of the sovereignty of God as any Stoic or Christian thinker could ask.[18] Where he differed from many was in his understanding of the *character* of that sovereignty. It was not obvious to Niebuhr, as it seems to have been to many in the Western politico-theological tradition, that divine sovereignty entails that (to use Harkness's language) "everything happens by the specific will and purpose of God." God's sovereignty is shown rather in the way God grants genuine existence and freedom to creatures, acts in and through their own free actions, freely bears the consequences of their doings and undoings, and continues to work creatively and redemptively with the world.

If we were to seek a precedent in Christian tradition for this understanding of God's patient and costly upholding of creaturely freedom, we might find more encouragement in pre-Constantinian and Eastern sources than in the dominant tradition of the Christian West, which has so heavily emphasized divine control.[19] Some more recent reflection by both Eastern and Western thinkers on the theme of divine power has gone back to the sources of the creedal affirmation of "God the Father Almighty." "Almighty" translates the Latin *omnipotens*, which is at best an ambiguous rendering of the Greek *pantokrator*. Jean-Pierre Batut explains: "Coined from the Greek verb *kratein* and an accusative pronoun, it [i.e., *pantokrator*] designates a permanent relation to the universe on God's part, and it could be translated as 'he who holds all things together.'"[20] Batut quotes the late second-century

17. See Philip Dixon, *"Nice and Hot Disputes": The Doctrine of the Trinity in the Seventeenth Century* (London: T. & T. Clark, 2003), and Michael Buckley, *At the Origins of Modern Atheism* (New Haven, CT: Yale University Press, 1987).

18. See Richard E. Crouter, "H. Richard Niebuhr and Stoicism," *Journal of Religious Ethics* 1 (1974): 129–46.

19. We might also look to certain careful rereadings of some central figures in that Western tradition itself, e.g., David Burrell on Aquinas.

20. Jean-Pierre Batut, "'God the Father Almighty': Thoughts on a Disputed Term," *Communio* 26 (1999): 278–94. The argument he outlines here is more fully developed in Batut, *Dieu le père tout-puissant* (Paris: Parole et Silence, 1998). See also the thorough treatment of the theme in Jan Bauke-Ruegg, *Die Allmacht Gottes* (Berlin: Walter de Gruyter, 1998), with the results more accessibly presented in his "Was heisst 'Ich glaube an den allmächtigen Gott'?" *Zeitschrift für Theologie und Kirche* 97 (2000): 46–79.

bishop Theophilus of Antioch: God is called *Pantokrator* "because he maintains (*kratei*) and contains (*emperiechei*) all things." In Batut's judgment, a better Latin rendition of the term than the problematic *omnipotens* (connoting "the Jovian possessor of an absolute power") would be *omnitenens*, "the one who holds all things"—a suggestion for which Batut is able to cite Augustine as precedent.[21] These investigations are consistent with Christopher Morse's observation, cited in chapter 4, that the character of God's action is consistent with the covenant promise embedded in creation and honored in the incarnation. Batut also takes care to point out that in these early formulations *pantokrator* is a title of the Father specifically and not a generic property of "deity." He notes that the later attribution of "almightiness" to all three persons, for example, in the so-called Athanasian Creed, tends to blur the distinctive meaning of *pantokrator* in a properly Christian account of God and of God's activity. The association of the providential theme of "upholding" or *sustentatio* with the Father, who bears—and bears with—all things, carries at least an echo of this earlier understanding.

Turning to the second theme of its Trinitarian exposition of God's activity, "God as Redeemer," the Calhoun Commission report cites two distinct but inseparable aspects of redemption: judgment and forgiveness, or justice and mercy: "Nowhere ought we expect to find the one without the other" (33).

Divine judgment as an aspect of redemption has both an ontic and a noetic dimension. Ontically, that is, with respect to events themselves, judgment is experienced in wartime when the human violation of God's good creation yields its terrible consequences. Because "*there is a natural and moral order of creation that God maintains against all man's wayward efforts*" (34), our waywardness leads to destruction. Yet it is not only perpetrators who are undone; the harm reaches far, and indiscriminately: "We see that in our world, the burden of suffering is not distributed according to guilt and innocence, but that all suffer, even the best" (39).

Accordingly, it is impossible to view war itself as intended by God. "It is not God's will that war shall come upon mankind, at any time,

---

21. Batut, "God the Father Almighty," 288–89.

nor that it be regarded as a suitable instrument for good" (35). War itself is not the judgment of God:

> It serves to reveal and vindicate the judgment of God that upholds inexorably the order of His world even though in the presence of that order some combinations of human decision and natural causation, in resistance to God's will for peace, bring war. . . .
>
> *Divine judgment is redemptive in purpose, and it becomes so in effect, as far as men are brought by its unceasing pressures to respond in repentance and faith.* (35–36)

War "serves to reveal and vindicate the judgment of God": this phrasing relates the noetic to the ontic dimension of that judgment. The calamity of war bears testimony to God's fidelity to creation and also to human infidelity to God and fellow creature. It reveals human idolatry, bringing human beings face to face with the inadequacy of their limited loyalties and commitments (34–35). The themes of repentance and faith introduced at this point also lead to the second aspect of God's redemptive relation to what is going on even in wartime, namely, mercy. Here too, as with judgment, one may distinguish an ontic and a noetic dimension. In what is going on, *"in the midst of the terrifying bitterness and hatred, deceit and disruption of war, there are signs of recreative forces at work it would seem continually"* (36). God's "purging, renovating, and reconciling power" is at work. New growth occurs; new relationships are formed; healing takes place. Accompanying these positive occurrences, as their noetic counterpart, are the *"searching insights into the meaning of human life and the will of God"* that war brings to some individuals (37). That is, war not only exposes our falsehoods, but in doing so may also lead to new apprehensions of truth.

Thus God relates redemptively to what goes on in wartime as both divine judgment and divine mercy are enacted and manifested in its events. The fact that God does so, and that therefore some good may emerge from the general destruction, does not by any means justify human resort to war (38). Just as with the section on "God the Creator," the report's treatment of "God the Redeemer"—or, as we might put it, of God's governance (*gubernatio*)—offers principles applicable to all situations and not simply to those of wartime. In everything that goes on, God's redeeming judgment and mercy are at work, directing creation toward its proper end. The character of this "directing" must be read in the light of the report's previous treatment of the character of God's "upholding" of creation, and of creaturely freedom and integrity; it is the same act viewed under two aspects.

The report takes up the third aspect of the divine action under the heading "God the Holy Spirit." "God as Life-Giver" would have been more consistent with the previous two headings, "God as Creator" and "God as Redeemer," as well as with the thematic intention of the whole. The inconsistency is probably inadvertent rather than deliberate. It is the life-giving work of God traditionally "appropriated" to the Holy Spirit that is the subject of attention here. "This aspect of His presence and action, once more, is not to be thought of as separate from His presence as Creator and as sovereign Redeemer. God is one, and His work is indivisible" (39).

In this, the briefest part of the report's doctrinal exposition, there is what appears to be a strange narrowing of focus. While the previous discussions of the work of God as Creator and Redeemer make it clear that these aspects of the divine activity pertain to all circumstances and all creatures, here the report concentrates on "a special range of peculiarly personal relationship between God and those men who actually respond to His presence in conscious trust. Through such men, God is able to perform works of power that are not possible in lives ruled by unbelief. This is in a special way the distinctive work of the Holy Spirit" (39–40). Several points are made in this connection. First, the report notes "the actual remaking of persons" through "the Spirit's work of sanctification" experienced in wartime as at other times. The "impulse" of the Spirit is one—"devoted love for God and man, and for all that is good, true, and right"; and the "gifts" of the Spirit are many, including "reinforced strength and courage, sharpened insight and self-forgetfulness, steadfast patience and serenity and joy, invincible security, and others too many to name. Including them all is an abiding experience of heightened, deepened, broadened fellowship with men and nature, and with God." This last observation leads to an affirmation that "the Holy Spirit is the living Ground of community. . . . Where the Spirit works, there diversity becomes enrichment of a common good rather than mere conflict or mutual destruction" (40).

There follows a carefully phrased discussion of the experiences reported by numerous Christians of "supernatural help and protection" or "unforeseen and powerful aid beyond known human powers" under the extreme circumstances of war.

> To the minds of many, these are palpable miracles in our time, like the "mighty works" that first century Christians took as signs and gifts of the Holy Spirit. Our problem now, like St. Paul's then, is to keep clear the right lines of Christian conviction across an area in which human cravings and emotions are uncommonly strong. It seems to us right to affirm that to every devoted person in war time, combatant or non-combatant, the presence of God offers an accessible source of power and spiritual security. Especially through genuine prayer, however inarticulate, a human spirit is opened toward God who is never absent, and strengthened to bear rightly whatever burden must be borne. That fresh energies, beyond the shallows drawn upon in ordinary living, can be tapped under conditions of great stress has long been known, and fresh testimony to the fact is welcome. Such energies, and such guidance as the hidden perceptions within men's bodies and minds may provide in times of extreme peril or exhaustion, can indeed manifest the watchful care of the God who neither slumbers nor sleeps. (41)

Moving more fully to the subject of prayer, the report seeks in the same way to distinguish a Christian understanding and practice of prayer from what "human cravings and emotions" might otherwise make of it. "We are assured that God will unfailingly provide, in answer to every one who turns to Him sincerely in prayer, the utmost of good that the attitude of the petitioner and the whole situation permit. But that good will often be very different from what the petitioner seeks" (42). While "humble prayer for safety or for bread can be real prayer . . . the models for prayer in time of trial are still the prayers in Gethsemane and on the cross" (42–43). "The one kind of petition, we believe, that God cannot accept as genuine prayer at all is a presumptuous and self-righteous effort to use Him and His power for human ends, chosen without regard to His will" (42).

This brief discussion of God as Life-Giver is remarkable for the way it combines subtle critique and reconstruction, aiming at a more adequate understanding of this aspect of the divine activity. However,

its overall shape is still dictated by a tendency in the churches' thinking to restrict the scope of the Spirit's influence to certain well-
demarcated areas mainly having to do with the inner life and
experience of believers, and to neglect the Spirit's indwelling and
vivifying of all creation.[22] If all of the important points it makes had
been made within the context of a fuller affirmation of what it means
for God to be Life-Giver as well as Creator and Redeemer in every
circumstance, with regard to the whole of creation, the report would
have come closer to realizing its promise as a reformulation of the
Christian doctrine of providence for our time.

In a passage from some later reflection on divine and human action
that seems to combine personal confession and Trinitarian insight, H.
Richard Niebuhr writes, "The action by which I am, is not one by
which I was thrown into existence at some past time to maintain
myself thereafter by my own power. It is the action whereby I am
now, so that it seems truer to say that I am being lived than that I
live."[23] Niebuhr does not mention the Holy Spirit, nor the notion of
the divine *concursus*, in connection with this remark. But clearly he
is speaking of a feature of existence not unique to him, nor even to
human beings, but one shared by all creatures. All creation is "being
lived," or "being being-ed": its life is a kind of participation in the
divine life. Against this background, the particular critical and constructive points made by the Calhoun Commission in this final seg-
ment of its doctrinal exposition emerge with greater clarity and
pertinence. However, the absence of a fuller account of this third
aspect of the divine action—the "concursive" aspect traditionally
associated with the Holy Spirit—is probably the greatest weakness of
the exposition. Once again, it is a weakness characteristic of mid-
twentieth-century Protestant theology, with causes traceable to early

---

22. For one recent corrective, see José Comblin, *The Holy Spirit and Liberation*, trans. Paul
Burns (Maryknoll, NY: Orbis Books, 1989).

23. H. Richard Niebuhr, *The Responsible Self*, ed. James M. Gustafson (New York: Harper
& Row, 1963), 114. Niebuhr was a profoundly Trinitarian thinker. His general and well-known
reticence about the Trinity, as about christology, stemmed more from an awareness of the difficulty of speaking rightly (e.g., nonidolatrously) on the doctrine in the contemporary intellectual and cultural climate than from any lack of commitment to its governing role in the
"grammar" of the Christian understanding of reality. The difficulty he faced in this regard was,
needless to say, also before the Calhoun Commission in its work.

modernity and perhaps even to late medieval nominalism. It is one point at which the Trinitarian vision the report aimed at was simply incapable of realization, given the circumstances in which the report was produced.[24]

Its limitations notwithstanding, in its pursuit of a christological and Trinitarian orientation this document articulates some decisive principles for a Christian doctrine of providence and offers us a model for doctrinal affirmation in our own time and place.

A Providential Piety

The American poet Robinson Jeffers (1887–1962) once likened Christianity to "strong poison in the sickly world" that "works yet for evil and good; medicinal / And deadly."[25] In Jeffers's sober judgment, expressed at various points throughout his poetic work, the deadly has far outweighed the medicinal in the long history of Christianity with Western civilization.[26] Several factors account for this outcome, but prominent among them in Jeffers's estimation is the encourage-ment Christianity has provided to human self-preoccupation. That human beings are God's particular concern, the pinnacle of God's creation and the special objects of God's providence, is in Jeffers's view a teaching that has had massively tragic consequences not only

---

24. In "The Concept of Providence in Modern Theology" (*The Journal of Religion* 43 [1963]) Langdon B. Gilkey sums up the situation thus: "About the most modern theology has been able to say is that (*a*) God preserves the being and the general order of creation within which naturally caused and freely willed particular events, and their consequences, occur—a doctrine of 'general providence'; (*b*) that God wills judgment and grace in relation to each his-torical event—a 'willing' through the Word and Spirit that relates in the present only to the inner life of believing men; and (*c*) that God somehow can 'bring good out of these evils he has not caused,' though how in the light of (*a*) this is to be understood if it involves more than (*b*) is never made clear" (179). Though the reference is somewhat garbled, the footnote to this pas-sage refers to the Calhoun Commission report as illustrative of its claim.

25. Robinson Jeffers, "The Year of Mourning," in *The Collected Poetry of Robinson Jeffers*, vol. 4, ed. Tim Hunt (Stanford, CA: Stanford University Press, 2000), 194.

26. James Karman's *Robinson Jeffers: Poet of California* (rev. ed.: Ashland, OR: Story Line Press, 2001) is a concise recent account of his life and work; on Jeffers's views on Christian-ity, see especially 99–100. William Everson's *The Excesses of God: Robinson Jeffers as a Reli-gious Figure* (Stanford, CA: Stanford University Press, 1988) is a valuable and provocative study of the theological vision in Jeffers's poetry.

for human beings themselves but also for their fellow creatures on earth. It is as if the incarnation backfired: rather than helping human beings get over themselves, it seems to have confirmed them in their own overweening self-estimate—or at any rate, its interpretation over the centuries in the context of the classical doctrine of providence seems to have done so.

In a summary of his own religious attitudes, expressed reluctantly in a letter to an inquirer, Jeffers wrote,

> I think it is our privilege and felicity to love God for his beauty, without claiming or expecting love from him. We are not important to him, but he to us.
>
> I think that one may contribute (ever so slightly) to the beauty of things. . . . But I would have each person realize that his contribution is not important, its success not really a matter for exultation nor its failure for mourning; the beauty of things is sufficient without him.[27]

Robinson Jeffers has been called the most theological of American poets. His judgment of the effects of Christianity in the West, and his articulation—hesitant and diffident in prose, forthright and powerful in lyric and narrative poetry—of his own decidedly nonanthropocentric vision of reality, are grounded in a piety that, however heterodox, has strong Christian elements. Jeffers's father was a Presbyterian minister and a seminary professor in biblical and historical theology; his mother counted Jonathan Edwards among her New England ancestors. Family prayers, Bible reading, and an atmosphere of respect for both theological and liberal learning shaped Jeffers's early years. His vision of the majesty and beauty of God, and at the same time of God's intimate indwelling of every atom of creation, is deeply rooted in the tradition in which he was raised. For Jeffers no less than for Jonathan Edwards, God is simply the most real, "the Being of beings," whose glory is evident in the sheer freedom and abundance of creation. The showing forth of this reality "calls forth our love and reverence."[28] For Jeffers, as for Edwards, our apprehension of the

---

27. Letter to Sister Mary James Power (October 1, 1934), in *The Selected Letters of Robinson Jeffers, 1897–1962*, ed. Ann N. Ridgeway (Baltimore, MD: Johns Hopkins Press, 1968), 221–22.

28. Robinson Jeffers, "Themes In My Poems" (1941), in Hunt, ed., *Collected Poetry*, vol. 4, 412.

divine beauty is (as Sang Hyun Lee says of Edwards) "not only an epistemic event but an ontological one."[29] Worship is the natural response—or it would be, if we could overcome the terror our own self-preoccupation prompts when we realize our own relative insignificance in this ongoing creative act, to say nothing of our *wrongness*, our being somehow out of true.

Worship requires, or, better, involves, a conversion. In Jeffers's view, the conversion is not merely from "self" but also from the collective ego of humankind; and this is one of the points at which, as he sees it, Christianity has typically failed its own vision. Not only egocentrism, but anthropocentrism—the unhealthy preoccupation of humanity with itself—must be decisively renounced. "I have fallen in love outward," Jeffers has one of his characters say, and by "outward" the speaker means that he has been attracted not merely to a good outside himself but more decisively to a good that transcends and radically decenters humanity.[30] Jeffers saw his work as expressing "a protest against human narcissism," and he could at times claim the Christian roots of this protest.

> Certainly humanity has claims, on all of us; we can best fulfil them by keeping our emotional sanity; and this by seeing beyond and around the human race.
>
> This is far from humanism; but it is, in fact, the Christian attitude:—to love God with all one's heart and soul, and one's neighbor as one's self:—as much as that, but as *little* as that.[31]

Though he believed that human beings "may contribute (ever so slightly) to the beauty of things," Jeffers actually held little hope for human redemption, that is, little hope that the deep wrongness in human beings might ever be overcome. The persistent fault in us may simply be an evolutionary fact, a concomitant of human consciousness and inextricable from it. In view of the immeasurable harm we do to

---

29. Sang Hyun Lee, "Edwards on God and Nature: Resources for Contemporary Theology," in *Edwards in Our Time*, ed. Sang Hyun Lee and Allen C. Guelzo (Grand Rapids: Wm. B. Eerdmans Publishing Co., 1999), 32.

30. Robinson Jeffers, "The Tower Beyond Tragedy," in *The Collected Poetry of Robinson Jeffers*, vol. 1, ed. Tim Hunt (Stanford, CA: Stanford University Press, 1988), 178. The character is Orestes.

31. Jeffers, "Themes," 412.

ourselves and to our fellow creatures, the extinction of our species was not, to Jeffers, an unwelcome prospect. The "inhumanism" of Jeffers's outlook—the term is his own, in contrast to "humanism"—does not signal a hatred of humanity but rather both a strong conviction that anthropocentrism is idolatry and a sorrowful acknowledgment that we are not likely to overcome it.

Jeffers's vision poses a serious challenge to any future Christian doctrine of providence. But it is a salutary challenge, one in which Christians may and should readily join. It provides an opportunity and suggests some resources for a badly needed radical correction: a kind of doctrinal *metanoia* in which we might die to an old understanding in which we have long been trapped and be made alive to a new, transformative possibility. Without that *metanoia*, a genuinely Christian doctrine of providence has no possibility of success, because providence in some guise will always be coopted to support what William Everson calls "our desperate hopes."[32] It will continue to be made to serve our felt needs for assurance and self-protection, providing the kind of "consolation" that Simone Weil rightly saw as antithetical to the gospel.

The anonymous fifteenth-century author of the *Theologia Germanica* puts the matter plainly:

> Some may say: "Now since God willeth and desireth and doth the best that may be to every one, He ought so to help each man and order things for him, that they should fall out according to his will and fulfil his desires, so that one might be a Pope, another a Bishop, and so forth." Be assured, he who helpeth a man to his own will, helpeth him to the worst that he can. For the more a man followeth after his own self-will, and self-will groweth in him, the farther off is he from God, the true Good [, for nothing burneth in hell but self-will. Therefore it hath been said, "Put off thine own will, and there will be no hell"]. Now God is very willing to help a man and bring him to that which is best in itself, and is of all things the best for man. But to this end, all self-will must depart, as we have said. And God would fain give man his help and counsel thereunto, for so

---

32. Brother Antoninus (William Everson), *Robinson Jeffers: Fragments of an Older Fury* (Berkeley, CA: Oyez, 1968), 12.

long as a man is seeking his own good, he doth not seek what is best for him, and will never find it. For a man's highest good would be and truly is, that he should not seek himself nor his own things, nor be his own end in any respect, either in things spiritual or things natural, but should seek only the praise and glory of God and His holy will. This doth God teach and admonish us.[33]

This unknown Christian writer shares with Jeffers a sense of the urgent necessity of a reorientation of our affections. There is also in his treatise evidence of a deep and joyous awareness of God's self-gift at the very core of all existence, human and otherwise.

God is the Being of all that are, and the Life of all that live, and the Wisdom of all the wise; for all things have their being more truly in God than in themselves, and also their powers, knowledge, life, and the rest; for if it were not so, God would not be all good. And thus all creatures are good.

. . . But what then is there which is contrary to God and hateful to Him? Nothing but Sin. But what is Sin? Mark this: Sin is nothing else than that the creature willeth otherwise than God willeth, and contrary to him.[34]

The human creature as such is good and has not been abandoned by God. To receive the gracious self-gift of God to humanity in Jesus Christ is to be enabled to "fall in love outward" (to use Jeffers's expression) and thus to experience a regeneration. To put off self-will is not to deny our worth and integrity but rather to affirm them at their source and to begin to recover them. This applies equally to the "collective self" of humankind and to our individual selves. Jeffers is more explicit than the author of the *Theologia Germanica* but certainly in continuity with him when he alerts us to the dangers of the collective egotism of nation, race—or species. But it is the older writer who testifies more clearly to the rebirth of hope that accompanies a radical

---

33. *Theologia Germanica,* ed. Thomas S. Kepler (Cleveland, OH: World Publishing Co. 1952), 121–22. The brackets are in the text quoted; they indicate material that is included in the most complete manuscript of the work (the Würzburg ms. of 1497) but is omitted from Martin Luther's edition. The critical edition is Wolfgang von Hinten, *"Der Franckforter"* (*Theologia Deutsch*): *Kritische Textausgabe* (Munich: Artemis Verlag, 1982), in which the quoted passage appears on 118–19.

34. *Theologia Germanica,* 125–26; Hinten ed., 120–21.

decentering of our desires, as we learn that "all our good is other than we thought."

An understanding of God's providence shaped by such considerations as these might well find apt expression in the words of Psalm 131:

> O LORD, my heart is not lifted up,
>   my eyes are not raised too high;
> I do not occupy myself with things
>   too great and too marvelous for me.
> But I have calmed and quieted my soul,
>   like a weaned child with its mother;
>   my soul is like the weaned child that is with me.
> O Israel, hope in the LORD
>   from this time on and forevermore.

Index